SURVIVAL MODE

A MEMOIR OF HOPE, LOVE AND SURVIVAL

THE TRUE STORY

OF A YOUNG MAN'S TRIUMPHANT JOURNEY
THROUGH LOSS, POOR GRADES, FAILURES, SETBACKS, DEPRESSION AND HOMELESSNESS.

JONATHAN EDISON

Crown Book Publishing
143 Cady Center suite #165
Northville, MI 48167

Manufactured in the United States of America

13 15 17 19 20 18 16 14

First Perennial paper back edition published 2014

Designed by Kendra Cagle

For information about special discounts for bulk purchases, please contact Edison Speaks International, 1-972-755-4231 or www.jonathanedison.com

---

The Library of Congress has catalogued the edition of this book as follows:
Edison, Jonathan Edward.
Survival Mode: a memoir of hope, love and survival/by Jonathan Edison -
1st edition Crown Publishing ed.
p. cm.
ISBN 978-1-4951-1375-8 (alk.paper)

1. Jonathan Edison. 2. Memoir-Biography 3. Survivors 4. African American boys 5. Michigan –Biography 6. Edison, Jonathan-Childhood youth 7. Teacher-Memoir 8. Overcoming obstacles-Professional 9. Grandmother's help 10. Detroit youth 11. Afro-American writers-Biography 12. Memoir-African American
Txu 1-904-337

Jonathan Edison

This memoir is dedicated to all
SURVIVORS -
OF CHALLENGES, STRUGGLES, PAIN,
SETBACKS AND OBSTACLES.

The fact that you're still here means-
You get another chance to get it right!
-Jonathan

To my Dad
Larry Edward Edison
R.I.P.,
your son, Jonathan.

JONATHAN EDISON

CONTENTS & CHAPTERS

JONATHAN EDISON

*"Struggles are required in order to survive in life,
because in order to stand up, you gotta know
what falling down is like."*

- HAPPYLIFE.COM

CHAPTER 1

The *Master* of the
GHETTO

*"Failure will never overtake me, if my desire
to succeed is strong enough."*

*"Strength does not come from physical capacity.
It comes from an indomitable will."*

-MAHATMA GANDHI

"Whannnnnnn," I cried.

"It's a boy!" the doctor exclaimed, as I, Jonathan Edward Edison, was born September 8, 1973 to Larry Edison and Glenda Horner of Detroit, Michigan, into what most statisticians and census bureau surveyors would consider the typical black American household. We lived with my grandmother in a small two-family apartment on Detroit's east side in the heart of what was known as "Black Bottom," surrounded by violence, prostitution, drug trafficking and the rodents that ruled the vacant lots on either side of our home. Dependent on welfare, creative budgeting, and the acclaimed "robbing Peter to pay Paul" school of finance management, we made do with a little and made a lot out of nothing. When it came to cooking, my grandmother was the most creative chef in the world; those guys on Chopped don't have anything on her. Some months she even rivaled the miracle of Jesus Christ himself when he turned five loaves of bread and two pieces of fish into a feast.

I remember many two-mile walks with my mother to the food stamp office when I was four years old. The hike didn't bother me at all. In fact, I enjoyed it. I always thought of it as an adventure, too young to understand that Indiana Jones would have been lucky to make it through my neighborhood. Instead of braving jungles filled with exotic foliage, we made our way through weeds that grew taller than my head. The temples of doom were burned out houses junkies used for shelter. The ancient ruins were abandoned cars, stripped, burned and left sitting on bricks like carcasses. The menacing shaman was the neighborhood bum loitering by the corner store, begging for change. The funny thing to me was no matter what day it happened to be, he always needed the same amount of money to "get me something to eat."

Outside the food stamp office, street hustlers, single mothers, and elderly people bought and sold food stamps like they were trading shares of stock on Wall Street. Standing in line, waiting patiently with my mother, I was always amazed by the number of people who relied on these little red, green, and white books that contained what looked like Monopoly money, and by the amount of brokering, trading, and wheeling and dealing that took place. I watched single mothers negotiate the sale of hundreds of dollars' worth of stamps for mere pennies on the dollar while their children cried and reached for them. My mom was often approached to sell her food stamps, but she always refused. She would simply say, "No, thank you. My little boy has to eat, look at how big his head is. I'd better keep some food in the house." The potential buyer would laugh and look down at me with my eyes as bright as California sunshine and say, "You're right, baby. This boy is growing. You two be careful out here."

We exited the food stamp office with $205 worth of food stamps, powdered eggs, canned beef and several bags of farina cereal, all meant to last us for an entire month. My mother always made sure I had something to carry, especially since she could tell helping out made me feel like a big boy. After she gave me my two bags of groceries, she always asked if they were too heavy. My reply was always the same, "No, Mama, I got it. Let's go. I'm ready."

As we began our trek back home, at first I whistled, skipped, and played superhero. I was He-Man, a.k.a. John-John, Master of the Ghetto. But gradually my little arms and legs would get tired. "Do you need to stop and rest?" Mama would ask. How could the Master of the Ghetto be tired? Under no condition would I stop walking, or put my bags down, because that would mean I wasn't a big boy, and that was the last thing I wanted. To me, life couldn't get any better—I had my mom, my dad, and the most loving grandmother in the world to nurture me and care for me. Our living situation was rare. Traditional family structures in Black Bottom was about as common as millionaires next door, which is to say, pretty much nonexistent. Considering the amount of love my mother expressed for my father and me, I found it difficult to understand how just one other individual could create such hell, cause so much destruction, and ultimately serve as the instrumental force in destroying my home, my happy family, and my relationship with my mother.

That individual's name was Donovan. He was my mother's high school sweetheart and first love. He was also the father of my mother's first two children, my half-siblings Marshall and Laurie. Donovan was a tall, smooth-talking man with deep hazel eyes, bronze-toned skin, perfect bone structure, and jet-black wavy hair he wore in a ponytail Sampson himself would envy. In the late '60s and early '70s, he was considered the Clark Gable of the ghetto. Although my mother seemed to love my father with all of her heart, that didn't erase the fact that Donovan was her first love. Donovan's hold on my mother ran deep into her soul, and she found it impossible to say no to him. It was as though he controlled her actions, her emotions, and her very will with his magnetic personality, winning smile, and mouth-watering beauty.

Donovan lived the fast life. He loved drugs, drinking, and stealing, just living life on the edge. He majored in car and merchandise theft, stealing vehicles from parking lots and appliances like toaster ovens and washers and dryers from large warehouses. His minor was petty theft with a concentration in small-change drug dealing. Donovan spent the majority of his time in jail, and at the same time plotting ways to superimpose his chosen lifestyle on my mother.

CHAPTER 2

The *Beginning* of the
END

*"There is no real ending. It's just the place
where you stop the story."*

-FRANK HERBERT

"Glenda, I'm missing $50 out of my wallet. Have you seen it?" my father asked my mother while getting dressed for his 7:00 a.m. shift as a pipefitter at the Detroit Water Board.

"No, honey, what $50? Are you sure you didn't spend it? Did it fall out of your wallet?" she said.

My father didn't protest. He just left for work with a look of bewilderment on his face. Little did he know that while he was at his second job the night before, my mother had used the $50 to bail Donovan out of jail.

As the weeks went on, it was obvious that my mother's mind was elsewhere. She wasn't the same energetic and vibrant mother I knew who was always up for my superhero adventures. She was tired all the time and had trouble staying focused. One morning in particular, as she attempted to make pancakes for the family, it became clear that something was really wrong. It was as if she had fallen asleep standing up over the hot stove cooking. She just stood there, staring into space, not moving or even blinking. As the pancakes burned and the kitchen filled with smoke, I sat at our small two-chair kitchenette and cried while my father and grandmother yelled at her. "What the hell is wrong with you? Are you high on something?"

She was high on something all right: Donovan's love and the continuous supply of pills he provided for her. When my father opened the back door to let the smoke escape from the kitchen, my mother still didn't respond. Instead, she stood there with a blank look on her face and a glazed look in her eyes that completely masked her usual charisma.

My mother's condition steadily worsened. My dad worked two minimum-wage jobs to support the family, whereas my mother's full time job was spending as much time as she could with Donovan behind my father's back. My mother would come home with cheap liquor on her breath and the strong odor of cigarettes in her clothes.

"Glenda, child, do you need some help?" my grandmother asked her one afternoon. "I'm worried about you, girl. You don't look so good."

"I'm fine," my mother said. "I've just been under a lot of pressure lately."

The pressure of trying to hide her feelings for Donovan was too much for her to bear, and she just lost it.

"Leave me alone! Just leave me alone!" she screamed. "I'm sick and tired of everyone asking me if I'm alright! I'm sick of this house, I'm sick of cleaning, I'm sick of cooking, I'm sick of that crazy boy running all around the house, I'm sick of your old behind, and I'm sick and tired of being sick and tired!"

I had never heard my mother talk like that before. What could this mean? She didn't love me anymore? Was I a bad kid? It's my fault, I thought. I dropped all of my marbles and ran to the kitchen in my Incredible Hulk pajamas.

"Mama, I'm sorry. Mama, I'm sorry. I promise, I'll be a good boy. I promise, Mama, I'll be good." My mother collapsed on the floor. I sat next to her, stroking her hair. "Mama, don't be sad, I'm going to be a big boy and help you, okay?" She looked at me with tears in her eyes, held me tight and kissed my forehead.

"Okay, you be a big boy and help your mama."

When my father came home from his second job at 1:00 a.m., he questioned her strange behavior and her outburst. Through the keyhole of their bedroom door, I nervously spied; I watched and listened as he asked her where she was during the day while I was at school, and for an explanation about the strange phone calls we received in the middle of the night. My mom made excuse after excuse, but none of them satisfied my father. He was no fool. He knew exactly what was going on and just wanted my mother to be honest with him in the name of love.

It had soon become common knowledge my mother had bailed Donovan out of jail and they were an item. Sadly, her relationship with Donovan only became more intense. They snuck around drinking and partying, while Donovan provided my mother with a steady supply of pills, heroin, and alcohol. With each week and each installment of pills, her drug problem grew worse and worse.

As the alcohol and drug abuse continued, my grandmother did everything she could to keep me in the dark about Donovan, my mother, and her drug habit. My mother's relationship with

Donovan progressed from casually hanging out during the day to two-week long excursions. They bounced from house to house and hotel to motel. Although my dad pretended to be unaffected by the turn of events in our household, it was destroying him inside.

One day, while my dad was working and my grandmother was sleeping, my mom decided to have a breakfast of pills followed by a bottle of Pink Champale. This day happened to be the first Saturday of the month, the day I looked forward to, the day we went on our adventure. She came in my room that morning at 7:00 and said, "Come on, John-John. Get ready, we're going to pick up our food stamps."

Ordinarily, I would have sprung out of bed, but my mother didn't look very well. Ten minutes later, she returned. "C'mon, boy, it's time to go, we don't want to be late," she slurred. "So get dressed and hurry up, darnit!"

Why was Mama talking funny? Was she all right? Maybe she was just sleepy, as she always seemed to be lately, I thought to myself. During the walk to the food stamp office, my mother could barely keep her head up.

She sat down on the curb outside the office. "Baby, give Mama a few minutes and we can go in, okay?" I sat with her. Strangers walked by us staring, shaking their heads and saying things like, "Look at her, she's high as the sky."

"Mama, are you okay? I'm ready to go! Come on, Mama, let's go! I'm ready to play superhero and be the Master of the Ghetto," I said.

"All right, baby, we can go," she said. As she stood up, I noticed she was swaying from side to side. She managed to make it into a corner store. While my mother paced the aisles, I wanted to get a sneak peek at my favorite superheroes in the comic books, and to possibly get my hands on a tasty bag of Andy Capp's Hot Fries. My mother asked if I wanted something.

"Yes, ma'am. I want these hot fries I found open on this rack," I said, with crumbs of hot fries all around my lips and in my mouth. "Found open!" I thought I was pretty slick.

"Boy, you think you're so smart, don't you?" she said.

She paid the clerk and turned to exit the store. Then, there he was: the most stunning man I had ever laid eyes on. He was so handsome, standing in the doorway wearing a tank top that showed off his rippling muscles and smooth chest. My mother stopped in her tracks, mesmerized by the man's presence. I couldn't stop staring at him either. He looked as if he should have been on the side of my Super Friends lunch box, posing as one of the new superheroes. Finally, I was face to face with Donovan.

"How're you doing, little boy?" he asked me.

"I'm not a little boy. I'm a big boy, right, Mama?" I fired back immediately.

I looked back to get her approval. She didn't hear me.

"Mama, let's go. Mama, I'm ready to go!" I shouted, pulling her hand.

Hastily, my mother gathered up our things and rushed to the door, pulling me along behind her. But there was one problem: the sleeve of my jacket was caught on the potato chip rack. I yelled for her to stop, but she didn't hear me, and the rack toppled over, dragging me with it. I hit the concrete floor, let out a scream, and blood poured from the right side my head.

My mother dropped the groceries. "Oh, my God! Somebody call an ambulance! My baby is hurt!"

The store clerk grabbed towels from his storeroom to stop the bleeding. Another customer held my hand and whispered in my ear, "You're going to be all right, little man, you're going to be all right." Donovan just stared at my mother as she tried her best to comfort and console her injured son.

After several minutes, we could hear the blaring sirens of an ambulance approaching in the distance. The emergency medical team rushed into the store and whisked me off to Children's Hospital located in Downtown Detroit. My mother watched over me as I lay on the stretcher in the back of the ambulance.

Her eyes were bloodshot from crying. The only thing I could think was I didn't know superheroes could bleed.

During the 15-minute ride to the emergency room, she must have said she was sorry a thousand times. The last thing she said as I was wheeled into the hospital was, "Baby, you're going to be fine, and Mama's going to be right here waiting on you, okay?"

"I know, Mama," I said faintly. "Everything is going to be okay because I'm a big boy and big boys are strong." That afternoon at Children's Hospital I received 36 stitches in my right eyebrow.

The following day, my grandmother decided she was not going to sit idly by and watch my mother destroy her son and grandson's lives. Still in pain from the fresh cut in my head, I listened to my grandmother and mother argue yet again, as they had so many times in recent months, about my mother's condition, her parenting skills, and how my grandmother didn't have any right to butt into her personal business. My mother professed that she was grown, free, and knew how to take care of her own son.

The more my mother pretended to be fine, the more her drug and alcohol abuse spiraled out of control. My father also pleaded with her to get herself cleaned up for the sake of our family, but his pleas were useless. She was a slave to Donovan's drugs and alcohol.

By age six and a half, I had grown numb to the constant fighting that seemed to lead to my mother disappearing for weeks. Even through all of the emotional hardships and sleepless nights, I still managed to be a pretty decent student in school. I realize now the reason I never wanted to miss school or even be late: I was trying to escape the reality of my negative home life. I yearned for security and stability. My family was falling apart, and I couldn't do a thing to prevent it. I couldn't control it and I couldn't stop it. Even with my superhero powers, this was too much for the Master of the Ghetto.

My mother drifted in and out of my life. Sometimes she managed to take me to school when my grandmother wasn't feeling up to the challenge. I remember a particular morning when my mother seemed to be in good spirits, sober to the best of my knowledge. She convinced my grandmother that she was doing okay and even made breakfast that morning the way she used to—pancakes, eggs, sausage, freshly squeezed orange juice, and plenty of syrup. Could it be that my mother was back?

"Hurry up and get ready for school. I know how you hate to be late," she said. I got myself ready for a brand new day of learning, seeing my friends and attending my favorite class, gym. Then I heard a car horn blow outside.

"There's our cab, John-John. Come on, let's go!" Mama said.

"I thought we were walking, Mama," I replied.

"Mama has to make a quick stop first, and then I'm going to drop you off at school, okay? It will only take a few minutes, I promise."

The cab headed down the main road for about twenty minutes, and then the driver made a sharp left turn into a pothole-strewn alley, lined with burned-out, boarded-up buildings and huge trucks. Flocks of pigeons circled overhead. Their droppings were splattered everywhere.

The cab came to a stop and my mother paid the driver. As soon as she opened the cab door, the vile smell of a slaughterhouse, burning trash from an incinerator, and the fumes from all of the trucks gave us a huge nasty kiss in the mouth and nose.

My mother walked towards a warehouse that looked condemned. Most of the windows were broken out; the back half was burned to a crisp and you could hear water dripping throughout it. I followed close behind her with my hands in my pockets. I didn't want to touch anything. My mother scaled the fire escape like Cat Woman all the way up to the third level. As I climbed up behind her, I wondered where we were going. I didn't see any doors.

She picked me up and shoved me through a window. I fell next to a bucket of human feces and urine. The stench was so revolting that I vomited down the front of my shirt. After my mother crawled through the window, she wiped my mouth and told me to go play. I wandered through a horrible room, across a rotting floor covered with pigeon and rat droppings, edging past openings where I could look down and see through to the ground floor. The only thing to sit on was a bare twin mattress with more urine stains on it than a hundred baby diapers. I decided to stand. Even in the daytime, this place was cold and dark.

I stood in the corner with my mouth covered. When I reached down to tie my shoe, to my surprise, there he was again. Only this time, Donovan didn't have the same twinkle in his eye. His existence didn't intimidate or engulf me, as it had during our first encounter. He was nervous, unsure of himself and desperate.

"Glenda! What took you so darn long? And why do you have this big head boy with you?" he asked.

"I had to pretend to be taking him to school, so I could make sure I had enough time to get the money from his daddy's stash."

Donovan took her money and returned with a lot of drugs and liquor. I was now an hour late for school, and my patience was growing thin.

"Mama, I'm ready to go to school!" I yelled. I turned the corner and saw my mother gobbling pills and drinking Pink Champale as if it were manna from heaven. As our eyes met, she said, "I better not ever catch you doing this. This is not good for you. You hear me talking to you, boy?"

"Yes, Mama," I said, watching in shock as Donovan ran his hands over my mother's body.

Two hours later, their party was over. Donovan went outside, hailed a cab and sent us on our way. During the cab ride, I could not look at my mother. Instead, I just stared out the window and listened to my mother drunkenly babble on and on. I wondered if my mother would ever get better. I was sad, scared, and confused, but I knew I had to be a big boy.

We arrived at school almost three hours late. My mother was so intoxicated she couldn't hold her head up. Her legs were like rubber and she was cursing everything from airports to zippers. My second grade teacher appeared and tried to assist her, but my mother refused.

"Jonathan, go on in and take your seat. I'll be there in a few minutes," my teacher told me. Once inside, I watched from the front door of the school. My teacher struggled to help my mother back into the cab. The tussle concluded with my mother vomiting all over my teacher's shiny black patent leather shoes. I burst into tears, ashamed of what had just happened.

"Jonathan, don't worry about that. You're a smart boy," my teacher said. As we walked down the hallway of the school, several of the other teachers had made their way out of their classrooms into the corridor to see what was going on. I overheard my teacher whispering to another teacher under her breath, "It's a shame, this boy is going to end up on drugs, dead, or in jail."

That afternoon, the principal called our house to tell my grandmother what transpired that morning. The principal explained that he felt it was in my best interests that my mother not be allowed to pick me up or drop me off anymore. Later on my dad picked me up from school. His face was deeply sad.

"How's my boy? How was school? Tell me what you learned today."

As I answered, he replied, "Oh, you're so smart." Through my dad's own personal pain and disappointment, he still managed to build me up, even though his heart was broken and his family was falling apart.

That night when my dad came home from his second job, he woke my mother up and told her she couldn't pick me up or drop me off at school anymore. My mother became irate. She started throwing things, yelling obscenities, and screaming that no one had the right to keep her from me. I covered my head with my pillows to drown out the sound of their voices, but it didn't work. Back and forth they argued. It felt like it went on for days.

Suddenly it stopped, so I jumped out of bed and peeked through my door. I couldn't see very well, but it looked as if my mother was lying face down on the floor. I ran over to her as fast as my little feet could carry me.

"Mama, get up! Mama, please get up!" I cried.

My father had reached his limit. He couldn't deal with it anymore. In the midst of the argument he had pushed my mother down onto the floor.

"That's it! Don't any man put his hands on me!" she screamed as she rose to her feet. I began to cry. I didn't know what was happening, but I knew it wasn't right or good. I didn't want her to go, but she ran into their bedroom and started shoving her things into a black hefty garbage bag. I ran after her.

"Mama, please don't go!" I shouted. "Please don't go, I promise I'll be good. I promise I'll be a big boy and won't cry! Mama, please!"

As she stormed down the steps, she said, "Don't you worry, John-John. It's going to be okay. Mama will be back for you, baby, real soon. I promise!"

CHAPTER 3
KIDNAPPED

"Et tu, Brute?"

-William Shakespeare

Early the next morning, my mother, Donovan, and two of his biker friends showed up at our house to rescue me from the clutches of my father and evil grandmother. Their motive was obvious: without me, my mother couldn't receive her food stamps or monthly ration of food. Therefore, in Donovan's eyes, I was the goose that laid the golden eggs that supplied the funds for his crime spree and drug habit. Somehow, my mother managed to sneak her way into the house and into my bedroom undetected by anyone.

I thought I was dreaming when she whispered in my ear, "John-John, John-John, wake up, wake up, baby." I opened my eyes and there she was standing over me with my jacket in her hand. "Baby, come on, let's go. Mama is taking you with her."

My grandmother just happened to wake up right then and spoil my mother's plan. She noticed the front door open and a black Chevy van parked outside our door and knew immediately what was going on. "Ed, get up!" she shouted to my father. "Glenda is trying to kidnap John-John!"

My father sprang from his bed, ran across the hall, and forced open my bedroom door. He told my mother she had five seconds to drop my clothes and leave our home before he called the police. "Leave now, Glenda! I mean it! You need to leave now!" he insisted. "John is not going with you under any condition. Get out, for the last time!" As my dad tried to remove my mother from my room, she began to scream.

"Glenda, are you alright? Do you need me to come up there?" It was Donovan, yelling from our front porch.

"If you don't want to die today, you better get the heck away from my door!" my father bellowed down the stairs. He turned to my mother. "You have the nerve to bring this gangster to my house to steal my son? I swear, if you don't get the heck out of here right now, someone is going to get hurt!"

The air was thick with aggression, hostility, and fear. My mother was adamant about taking me with her, even after my father's thunderous warning. She gathered up as many of my clothes as she could and snatched me out of bed. Barefoot and in pajamas, I watched my mother stare down my father. She pulled me close to her side and strolled through the hallway like nothing was going on. My grandmother, armed with her cane made of solid oak, met us near the kitchen.

"Glenda, I'm telling you right now, you'd better let my grandbaby go or I'm going upside your head so hard with this cane that my new middle name is going to be 'Hit' em Hard Hoe!'" my grandmother threatened. "I don't want to hurt you, Glenda. Just let him go! He doesn't belong to you and he's not going with you!"

"I'm taking my baby with me no matter what anybody says or does!" my mother shrieked. "He's my son and he belongs to me!"

I didn't know who to side with. I loved my mother and I wanted to go with her, but I knew she wasn't well. I loved my granny and I wanted to stay with her, but my granny and my mother were cursing at each other. I loved my father and I wanted to stay with him, but I could see in his eyes that he didn't love my mother anymore.

"Glenda, let him go! Let him go NOW!" my father yelled again.

"Hey man! Stop yelling at my woman! Glenda, get that boy and let's go!" Donovan yelled. The standoff had reached its peak. As I stood in the middle of this twisted love affair, caught up in a typhoon of anger, confusion, and insanity, I just closed my eyes. I shut everything out and pretended that it was a bright, sunny Saturday morning and I was on my journey to the food stamp office. I was whistling, having fun and playing superhero, protecting the ghetto from evildoers.

Suddenly, my mother grabbed me tight, dropped my clothes and charged towards the front door. My grandmother swung her cane, missing my mother by only inches, hitting me on the top of the head instead. With me tucked under her arm like a football, my mother tried her best Jim Brown move, but it didn't work on my father, a six-foot-two, 250 lb. All-American athlete and former soldier. My father grabbed me out of my mother's arms, sending her in a spin. With me in one hand, he pushed her out the front door and down the porch stairs. Lucky for her, Donovan was there to break her fall.

My mother still wasn't done. She charged back up the stairs after me. Before my father could react, my mother lunged out and grabbed the bottom of my pajama pants. Donovan ran up the stairs after my mother and helped her pull me down the stairs with them. At this point, the mental and physical stress on my small frame was unbearable, and I passed out from hysteria.

At the end of the tug-of-war, my father and grandmother prevailed. Of course, my mother wasn't happy with that outcome. When I regained consciousness, I could hear her outside in the street, yelling at the top of her lungs about how she loved me and how she was never going to leave me. Forty-five minutes later, Donovan decided enough was enough. He forced my mother into the van. "I'm coming back for my baby! I'm coming back for you! He's mine, he's mine!" she screamed, as they sped away.

I felt like I had been run over by a truck. My head was throbbing, my ankle was bruised and two of the fingers on my left hand were sprained. The pain was worse than when I fell in the store and had to get stitches. As I lay on my bed, I looked over to my dresser and caught a glimpse of my Super Friends lunch box. "I'm getting out of the superhero business," I thought. "There's too much pain involved."

In the calm after the storm, we tried to pick up the pieces and move on with our lives. My dad went to work, and my grandmother sat in the kitchen listening to the news on her small clock radio while she drank her morning cup of coffee.

Nevertheless, as much as we pretended things were normal, it was difficult for all of us. My mother was an indispensable part of the puzzle, and we missed her love.

As time went by, the love I had for my mother grew even stronger. Many nights, I cried myself to sleep because I wanted to be near her. Who was going to walk with me to the food stamp office now? Who was going to make my breakfast the way she did? I developed a severe case of chronic bedwetting. As soon as I closed my eyes to go to sleep, I would wet myself. I didn't know what was wrong with me. I tried to drink little or nothing before bedtime. Unfortunately, it did nothing to remedy the situation, and I was too embarrassed to tell my father. What would he do, if he knew his only son was a bed wetter? I could not confide in my grandmother either, because I knew she would have told my father. Initially, I tried the old "change the sheets and flip the mattress over" routine, early in the morning before anyone woke up, but I was wetting the bed so much that my mattress, my room, and my superhero pajamas began to reek.

After a week or so, my secret was discovered. My dad was getting ready for work, when he decided to come into my bedroom and go over my homework with me. When he opened the door, he found me butt-naked holding my mattress, standing in a pile of smelly sheets and pajamas. He didn't get upset. He had a temper when it came to foolishness, but on this occasion he was very understanding.

"John, what's bothering you?" He asked gently.

I explained to him as plainly as a seven-year-old could that I couldn't stop wetting my bed and I missed my mother. My father stood frozen in the doorway in silence. His eyes swelled with tears. I looked at him in bewilderment. I'd never seen my father cry before. I didn't even know he could cry. To me, my father was invincible. I ran and jumped into his arms, and though no more words were exchanged, something amazing happened that morning as a result of us both being vulnerable and transparent. Quietly, he carried me to the bathroom to get ready for school, and in that moment I knew that my Dad loved me more than anything on this earth. It felt like we had forged an unbreakable bond.

After my dad helped get me ready for school that morning, our relationship was never the same. My father began to pay more attention to me, and tried his best to make sure that my emotional needs were met. For the most part, I was a pretty happy kid that loved life, and after my Dad saw me so upset, his heart softened and he was forced to parent me differently. Pretty soon after that, my father started a tradition with me that I have established with my own kids. No matter the weather, rain, sleet, snow or sunshine, my father without fail would take me to two special places every Saturday. The first place we went was a matinee movie and then we would visit my favorite place on earth, the Golden Arches in the Sky, A.K.A. McDonald's.

My grandmother cooked every day and I mean every day. Oh, what a treat it was to spend an afternoon with my Dad at McDonald's! In the late '70s and early '80s, there weren't many safe havens in the African-American community besides church, the Salvation Army, and school. And people in my community, including my family, very rarely ate out or went to restaurants. If you could afford to go to McDonald's any time of the month, it was a big freaking deal. So for me, our Saturday outings to McDonald's were the equivalent of getting dressed up in a beautiful tuxedo and taking a limo to a five-star restaurant for a 5oz. filet steak dinner with all the trimmings, coffee, and dessert. I will never forget the countless moments that we shared underneath those golden arches. This was our exclusive time to talk, to laugh, to explore, to think, to share, to communicate, to open up, and sometimes just be silent in each other's presence.

I ordered the same thing every time—cheeseburger no mustard, fries, orange drink, and a hot apple pie. We tried to always sit in the same booth or at least the same area each time we visited. After about the third Saturday in a row, everyone on the lunch shift knew exactly who we were, kind of like Norm in Cheers—it felt great! When I walked through the doors of the McDonald's with my dad close behind me, I felt like I was ten feet tall. I knew from talking to my friends in my neighborhood that most of their dads weren't around. In some cases, they hadn't even met them before. So for me to be with my pops was a real treat.

On our Saturdays at McDonald's we would talk about everything, but no matter what we discussed, he always allowed me to take the lead of the conversation. I never wanted to talk about my mother, and he didn't force it on me. My favorite subject of all time to discuss with him was school. School for me was great. I loved my teachers, I loved my class and I really loved being one of the smartest kids in school. By the second semester of the third grade, not only had I made the honor roll, I had perfect attendance too. My grandmother and father were so proud of me. My life was improving—the bedwetting problem was at a minimum, I had a firm grip on who I was, and I understood how much love was still in my home. I was finally big enough to walk to school by myself, and had become somewhat of a celebrity for being the only kid in school with perfect attendance. The other kids, the teachers, even my neighbors joked you could set your watch by me, because I was always on time.

Then, the happiness and confidence that my father and grandmother worked so hard to instill in my world and around me came grinding to a halt when my mother and Donovan invited themselves back into my life.

It was a normal Thursday afternoon at Tendler Elementary School around 2:45 p.m. My classmates and I were putting away our supplies and gathering up our belongings in preparation for our short walk home. Ms. Thomas, my third grade teacher, was busy passing out treats as she always did for the students who modeled good behavior that day. As I cleared my desk and packed away my multiplication flash cards, the school secretary called down to my classroom over the intercom.

"Please excuse the interruption, Ms. Thomas. Can you send Jonathan to the office? His ride is here to pick him up."

Ms. Thomas gave me a treat and a hug, then handed me three sheets of homework and sent me on my way. I wondered who was picking me up early and why.

When I arrived at the main office, I saw a lady in a long black trench coat having a conversation with the school secretary. The woman's voice sounded familiar and as I got closer, I realized it was my mother, wearing dark sunglasses, and holding a bag of Andy Capp's Hot Fries in her hand.

"Come on, baby, let's go home," she said, dangling the bag of chips in front of me.

I didn't know how to react or what to say. What should I do? I was afraid of her, but I also loved her. I didn't want to see her, but I really had missed her. In the end, I went with her.

As we walked towards the front door of the school, she stopped, kneeled down to face me, and told me how much she loved me. She also said that she and my dad were back together again and he had told her to pick me up. Naturally I believed her.

Happily I took her hand and we walked out of the school together. We climbed into the taxi that was waiting for us. I was so excited at the idea of us being a happy family again. I couldn't wait to see the look on my father's face when he got home from work. With a smile as big as the Grand Canyon, I turned to my mother and shouted, "I love you, Mama!" She didn't respond, just rocked back and forth. I noticed that she seemed very nervous, and she kept turning around, looking through the back window of the cab.

I looked over at her again and yelled, "Mama, aren't you happy? Mama, aren't you happy? Come on, get happy, Mama!"

My mother snatched the dark sunglasses off her face. "Boy, shut up! Shut up!" she cried. "Just for one minute, will you? I can't think and you're making me nervous. So be a good boy and be quiet!"

In shock and disappointment, I slumped down in my seat and stared out the window. As the cab made its way through the city, I realized that none of the scenery looked familiar.

"Mama, where are we going? This isn't the way home."

"Boy, didn't I tell you to be quiet? It's a surprise, okay? Now sit back, relax, and shut up!"

The cab made a sharp right turn onto a narrow street. That's when I knew where we were going. It was the same place we had been that horrible day I was late for school. As the cab driver pulled closer to the warehouse, fear consumed me. I couldn't believe that my mother would expose me to such an evil and filthy place again. But there we were, making that climb up the fire escape and through the window that led to hell.

Once we were inside, my eyes began to tear up from the horrible fumes. I went into a violent sneezing fit from all the dust. When the spell passed, I saw approximately 50 or 60 large boxes with pictures of televisions on the side of them taking up most of the warehouse.

I followed my mother as she maneuvered her way to the back, near an open window facing the street. I heard loud, deep voices. It was Donovan and his two motorcycle buddies. Villains dressed in dark clothes and dark sunglasses? This was a job for the Master of the Ghetto. In my head I just really wanted things to end, and I imagined myself as Master of the Ghetto to make the situation better.

I stood back and watched as they celebrated a job well done. I learned later that earlier that morning, the three of them had broken into Fretter's Appliance store and cleaned them out. Donovan and his gang had managed to get away with approximately fifty 32-inch color television sets. Donovan approached me, asking for a high-five. I just stared a hole through him with my x-ray heat vision. I was no longer in awe of him, nor was I afraid of him, my mother, or anything else. With my heart pumping and my adrenaline at full throttle, I pushed my chest out and shouted at Donovan, "You'd better take me home right now, punk! Or I'm going to call my father and you know he will come and kick your butt!"

Donovan and his biker buddies thought my tirade was hilarious. They joked about me being tough enough to join their gang, until I surprised Donovan with a technique my gym teacher taught us to use if a stranger ever tried to grab or hurt us. I shot

Donovan a straight right jab to his groin and hit him so hard that I put him on his knees.

Silence fell over the entire room. I stood over Donovan, waiting to hit him again. For a moment my mother glared at me as if she couldn't believe what I had just done, and then she pushed me out of the way and ran over to Donovan. Embarrassed, with tears of pain in his eyes, he started swearing and yelling at me, describing what he was going to do to me. I didn't care anymore. I stood my ground.

Once the commotion settled down, I saw that it was dark outside. I could smell rain in the air. I told my mother that I wanted to go home, but my cries fell on deaf ears. I sulked and sat dejectedly in a corner of the warehouse. I watched Donovan and my mother do drugs, drink, and argue about where I was going to sleep. Donovan eventually removed two of the televisions from the boxes, crushed the cardboard down, and threw them on the floor for me.

"Here! Sleep on this. If you make a sound or try to run away, I'm going to whoop your little butt!" His mouth was tough, but as I had discovered, his private parts were tender. Donovan and my mother cuddled up and fell asleep on a filthy bare mattress next to the window.

Of course I couldn't sleep. I was tired, hungry, cold, and irritated. I just wanted to go home. Exhausted, I finally dozed off for a couple of hours, hoping to wake from this tortuous nightmare safe and sound and in my own comfortable, warm bed.

Around 7:00 a.m., my eyes popped open like clockwork. Unfortunately, the morning brought no relief; I was still in the hellhole of the vile warehouse. I rushed over to where Donovan and my mother were sleeping and gently nudged her. I anxiously whispered in her ear, "Mama, I'm ready to go to school." She didn't budge, so I kept pestering her. After a few minutes, she finally rolled over and asked what I wanted.

"Mama, please take me to school. I'm ready to go to school. I can't be late! I can't be late!" I yelled frantically. My mother looked at me hazily. "You're not going to school today," she said. She rolled over and went back to sleep.

My mouth and will had become more powerful than ever before. "What the hell do you mean, I'm not going to school today?" I cursed her. "Yes, I am! I'm leaving right now!"

I ran back to the other side of the warehouse and grabbed my book bag. I put on my shoes and raced toward the window. I threw my bag out the window. Just as I got my left leg and half my body onto the fire escape, Donovan grabbed me by the back of my shirt and threw me on the floor. He swore and threatened me again, this time from a safe distance. I looked over at my mother and she didn't say a word. She just watched him yell at me as if he was my father. What was wrong with her?

Donovan and my mother continued to hold me hostage in their den of evil. They wouldn't allow me to go to school or even outside for fresh air. My diet consisted of sardines, peanut butter, canned meat and potato chips. I had nowhere to brush my teeth, bathe, or go to the bathroom. I had to do number two into an old red chitterling bucket that was placed down at the other end of the warehouse. The worst part was that Donovan forced me to empty the bucket every time I used it out of the window onto the ground. It was disgusting! After about a week flies were buzzing everywhere around the pile of feces. During the day there wasn't much to do to occupy my time, so I just rattled off numbers, facts and figures all day to myself. I recited states and capitals, multiplication tables, and counted by twos, then threes, then fours. . . . I used my imagination to teleport myself back into Ms. Thomas's room and pretended that I was in class. I sat up tall on the floor, crossed my legs and pretended that the wall was her chalkboard. I even raised my hand like she instructed us to do when I imagined she was calling on me to answer a question.

At night I did my best to steer clear of Donavan, because that's when he seemed to be at his worst—cursing loud, acting reckless and threating my mother. I watched him treat my mother like a second-class citizen and talk to her in a demeaning and cynical way. He knew how to yank the "esteem" right out of my mother's soul. He had her wrapped around his little finger, he knew it, and there was nothing that anyone could do about it. As the days went by, I watched my mother shake, nod, and trip over furniture because she was so out of it. The days ran into each other. My concept of time was thrown off and all I wanted to do was go home. The one thing that I didn't do that entire time was cry, because I wasn't scared, I was furious! Some days I even thought about smashing Donovan into little pieces like one of my favorite heroes, the Incredible Hulk. If only I could turn green and burst out of my shirt!

Thanks to an anonymous tip, sixteen days after my kidnapping, my prayers were answered. In the middle of the night, the sound of sirens and then footsteps filled the air. A swarm of angels dressed in police uniforms stormed the warehouse with their weapons drawn. They found Donovan and my mother passed out on the floor and me shivering and curled up in the corner. An officer took off his coat, wrapped it around me, and picked me up. After the handcuffs were slapped on Donovan, the police questioned my mother for several minutes. My mother was also arrested that day. I watched as they placed the handcuffs on her and forced her into the back of the squad car. The funny thing was she never looked up. Not once did she turn around to see if I was ok. I stood in the middle of the street and watched as they drove her away, sirens blaring and lights flashing.

An officer took me to the station, where I saw my mother in custody in an interview room. She boo-hooed and dropped a few tears, eventually convincing the officers that Donovan was holding both of us against our will. They were about to release me back to her, but when I overheard one officer telling another that I could go back home with my mother, I yelled, "I want to go home! I want to go home! I'm not going with her, please don't make me go with her!"

The officer was shocked. He just stared at me. Why wouldn't a little boy want to go with his mother?

"Son, do you know your address?" he asked.

In one breath I blurted and recited everything I knew: *"Yes sir, I live at 2925 Lycaste, my phone number is 313-822-0643, my father's name is Larry, my grandmother's name is Granny, I'm eight years old, I'm in the third grade, and my teacher's name is Ms. Thomas. I go to Tendler Elementary School, I'm on the honor roll, I'm never late or tardy, my name is Jonathan Horner, my nickname is John-John, my favorite color is blue and I'm the Master of the Ghetto."*

The officers came over one by one to check on me while we waited, but all I could see were their lips moving. The only sound I wanted to hear was my grandmother's and my father's voice. Finally, I saw my dad's dark brown Ford Zephyr pull up. He ran around to the car to help my grandmother out. The police tried to hold me back because they had not identified Granny and Dad as my family. But when my grandmother looked at the two police officers that were holding on to me they immediately let me go. I ran over to her like my shoes had warp speed and she hugged me so tight that I could barely breathe. Finally, I was safe and free to go home. The moment I buckled my seat belt, I was out cold like I had been working the graveyard shift digging ditches. When I woke up the next morning, I was in my superhero pajamas, and before my feet hit the floor my nose picked up the most wonderful scent that I have ever smelled. It was the sweet smell of bacon, eggs, and pancakes cooking in my grandmother's kitchen! If heaven had a basement, this is where it was!

Donovan was eventually charged with grand theft larceny, child endangerment and sentenced to three to five years in prison for violating the provisions of his probation. My mother was released and let off with a warning, and only the stipulation that she had to check herself into a rehabilitation center 30 days after her arrest. But even though Donovan's physical body was incarcerated, the evil spirits of his drug addiction and alcohol abuse lingered and lived in my mother's world for many more years to come.

CHAPTER 4

Scared Half to *Death*
(TWICE)

"Courage is being scared to death….
but saddling up anyway"

-JOHN WAYNE

By the time I reached the fifth grade, I was doing well in school, and my life was stable. My dad changed my last name from Horner to Edison to give me a fresh start. I was heavily involved in sports, and went to church every week with my grandmother.

My dad had moved on with his life. He began dating our next-door neighbor's daughter Tanzella. My father was smitten with her from the very beginning. They married a few years later. They are still married with two beautiful children, Starmaine and Demetrius.

My dad was also able to find a more stable job that paid him enough to quit his second job. His new position was with Federal Mogul, and although the money was great, it required him to work outdoors in the elements. His hours were shorter, but his workload was grueling. He would leave for work at 7:30 a.m. and get off at 4:30 p.m., but once he got home, he would sleep straight through dinner til almost 10:00 p.m. every night.

My routine after school was simple and precise. Every day after school, I ran home, made a bologna and cheese sandwich, changed my clothes, did my homework and then grabbed my basketball, football or bike, and headed out the front door. The afternoon's sport of choice depended on what was going on in my neighborhood. Sometimes, I would take my basketball to the alley across the street from my house and shoot hoops for hours with my best friends, Otis and Donnie. Other times, if I was feeling a bit more dare-devilish and adventurous, I would ride my bike up and down the street, popping as many wheelies as I could, trying to beat my record, which was twelve.

On one particularly hot afternoon in May after school, I saw Otis and Donnie with Ki-Ki, Kawana, and Nikka playing an intense game of tag. I ran down the street to join in the fun.

Because our parents repeatedly told us not to play in the street, we played in the vacant lot next door to Ms. Johnson's house. Ms. Johnson was Donnie's grandmother and a really nice lady. She always made us cookies and gave us soft drinks in the summertime. She was infatuated with big German shepherd dogs, and kept five of them chained in her backyard to keep intruders out. The best thing about Ms. Johnson's vacant lot was there was an old 1970 Chevrolet El Camino sitting in the middle of the lot, stripped down and left for dead.

That afternoon, we played until the sun went down. Around 8:00 p.m., we decided to roll out the hose from the side of Ms. Johnson's house to take a water break. The boys grabbed the hose and, of course, we began spraying the girls with it. Soon we had created a mud moat around the old car. Donnie rolled up the hose and we began to play tag again. I was it. I started chasing everyone around the car again, slipping and sloshing through the mud.

Suddenly everyone jumped on top of the car.

"No fair!" I yelled.

"Look out, look out, look out! Look out, John!" the girls screamed. "Run! He's right behind you!"

I wondered who I was supposed to run from, and then I heard a loud bark. One of Ms. Johnson's German shepherds had gnawed through his chain and sprang over the fence.

I tried to jump up on the hood of the car, but I wasn't quick enough. The German shepherd took one gigantic leap and dug his claws in my back. He knocked me back down into the mud, biting, scratching, and tossing me around like a rag doll.

My friends screamed as the dog mauled me. The dog was relentless. When I was able to break free for a moment, I kicked it in the face. It almost worked, but he jumped on my back, pinning me down on the ground. His jaws clenched down on my left leg, ripping it to shreds as I howled for help.

Suddenly, another angel from God, Donnie's Uncle Kenny, heard me screaming and beat the dog off with a baseball bat. My entire body was covered in blood, dog saliva, puncture wounds, and mud. There was blood streaming from my head, back, face, neck, and leg. I could barely see or hear anything. I was conscious, but everything around me was moving in slow motion. The girls raced up the block to my house to tell my dad and grandmother what had just occurred.

My grandmother secured me in the back seat of my dad's car and we raced to the hospital. Surprisingly, I was really calm during the drive over. Yes, I was in a lot of pain but my grandmother held me tight and whispered how much she loved me. Those words alone were more powerful than any trauma that I could ever face.

Once we arrived at the hospital the nurses rushed me into the trauma center and two doctors began working on me immediately. I required two skin grafts and 160 stitches to my left leg.

I remember the nurse taking photos of my leg in the emergency room, and you could see clear to the bone from where the dog had torn away the flesh. The muscle in my left calf was severely damaged, and the doctors were concerned that I would have to wear a brace on my leg for the rest of my life. I was in a wheel chair for three months while my leg healed, and then did physical therapy twice a week for the next three years. I got rid of the brace shortly after that.

I thank Kenny Bell every day in my prayers for saving my life.

In the middle of sixth grade, my father sat me down and told me I was going to have to start being more mature as I entered into manhood. I had just stopped wetting the bed and wearing superhero pajamas. He explained to me that all responsible men knew how to take care of themselves. I listened, but really I had no clue what he was talking about.

The next week, the lessons began: Cooking and Cleaning 101. Early Saturday morning at the crack of dawn, my dad woke me up out of a sound sleep. He handed me a bucket, a mop, a broom, a dust pan, a can of Ajax, a bottle of Pine Sol, three rags, and a three-pack of yellow latex gloves.

"Let's hit it!" he said.

That morning I wiped, cleaned, scoured, and mopped everything in the house that had a surface on it. By 11:00 a.m., I was exhausted and couldn't wait to peel off the soaked latex gloves. My clothes stuck to my body like glue from all the sweat and dirty water. My hands were pale from constantly dunking them into buckets of hot, soapy water. At 7:00 p.m., I was finally released from duty. Shortly afterward, my dad came into my room and asked me if I had learned anything that day. I was tired. I just nodded and replied, "Yes, sir. I learned a lot." Then I climbed in bed and slept right through dinner and into the next day. I didn't wake up until it was time for church the next morning.

After church, I came home to find my father waiting in the kitchen for me with an apron, a towel, a potato peeler and a 50 lb. sack of Idaho potatoes. One by one, I peeled and peeled and peeled those potatoes as my dad remained completely silent, just towering over me and watching to see whether I would finish. It took hours. When I got down to the bottom of the bag, my hands had cramped up. Still, I didn't complain, even though I was mad at him for making me peel all those freaking potatoes. When I finished, I turned around to see the look on his face, but discovered he was no longer there. I ran out of the kitchen to search for him and found him leisurely lying in bed, watching television. I was really furious then, but before I could say anything, he looked at me and said, "Good job, son. Now go and get cleaned up." After several weeks of Basic Training 101, I quickly progressed from peeling potatoes to baking homemade rolls.

By the time I was in the seventh grade, I could cook and clean as well as a professional chef or housekeeper. I later figured out that my dad's mission was to groom me into being a completely self-sufficient young man. He achieved his goal, because by the summer of that year, I had completely taken over the housekeeping duties, and my main focus was taking care of my grandmother. Although she was well enough at that time to move around, I could see that her health was beginning to diminish. I cooked all of our meals, ran her errands, and still managed to play Little League basketball for the Detroit PAL "Run & Guns" with coaches Mike Quick and Bobbie Johnson three days a week.

My granny Cloraine Marie Turner was my entire world. To me, she was the most incredible woman on the planet. She was strong, tough, straightforward, and could hold her own with the best of them. Telling stories, playing cards, telling jokes, you name it she could do it. Not only was she tough, she was also very in tune with everything around her, which gave her a lot of wisdom and insight into people's characters. Most importantly, she loved me unconditionally and took care of me as if I was her son. Regardless of the mistakes I made, she never criticized me or beat me down verbally. She may have popped me upside the head with her cane every now and then, but we were absolutely inseparable. My first bout with the chickenpox, she was there. The night my temperature shot up to 103 degrees, she was there. The day neighborhood bullies jumped on me after school, she was there. The nights I had nightmares about my mother and couldn't get back to sleep, she was there. When I accidentally set my dad's bed on fire, she was there. The Sunday I ran out of church in fear because a woman next to me caught the Holy Ghost, she was there. When I decided I was grown and challenged my father to a fistfight, she was there, thank God. I loved her with every ounce of my soul.

The eighth-grade school year started off with a bang. The Chrysler Corporation notified us that they were buying the property in our area and converting it into a Chrysler Jeep Plant. This was good news, because it meant that they were going to pay off our old house and move us into a brand new home in a different part of town. To top things off, a few weeks later, I was hit with the best news of my life. I received a letter of acceptance to Cass Technical High School, one of the premier high schools in Detroit. My grandmother and father were so proud of me because only the brightest and most promising students were accepted to Cass Technical High School. My Granny was especially proud of me and couldn't believe that her little grandson was on his way to high school.

In May, we moved to Detroit's east side, near 7 Mile and Mound Road into a beautiful house in a peaceful neighborhood. My dad kept a room at our house, but ultimately, he moved in with his new wife Tanzella. I missed my Dad terribly, but I made the best of it. Not only did I have a new home, a new set of friends and a spot on the roster at Cass Technical High School, I even found a summer job at Bob & Don's Meat Market around the corner from my house. I worked a couple of days a week, played basketball until the sun went down, and took care of my grandmother. Life was good again.

The summer that year was extremely hot, and unfortunately, our house was not equipped with air conditioning. This was a problem for my grandmother, who had recently suffered a mild stroke, and frequently experienced shortness of breath and hot flashes. Yet as always, we made do with what we had, so I rigged a fan and secured it in her bedroom window to help keep her cool. Every day before I left the house to practice my game, I would check on my grandmother to see if she was hungry or if she needed anything: a glass of water, her medicine, some food, or a cold towel for her head.

One day in August, the temperature reached well over 100 degrees. When I went in to check on my grandmother around lunchtime, she didn't look so good, but she said she was fine and all she needed was a piece of fruit and a glass of water. I fetched them for her and then went back to my room. At 6:00 p.m., after watching all of the television I could tolerate, I slipped on my basketball shorts and headed down the hall to look in on her one more time before leaving the house.

"Hey, Granny! Do you want something to eat right now or do you want to wait until I get back?" Honestly, I was hoping she would say that she could wait until I got back, because I couldn't stand being cooped up in the house one more second.

"Yes, son. Make your granny something to eat right now before you go."

"Okay," I replied. "What do you feel like having today?"

She smiled and said, "Granny's kind of hungry today. I feel like I want meatballs smothered in gravy, white rice, cabbage, black-eyed peas, cornbread muffins, and walnut brownies for dessert."

My jaw hit the floor. "Are you sure, Granny? That seems like a lot of food."

She just smiled and nodded. I went to the kitchen without hesitation to get dinner started for her. I was in the middle of making gravy when there was a knock at my side door. It was three of my new buddies, Richard, Pete, and Malcolm who lived down the street. They were basketball fanatics like me. I slapped a few hands, and told them I would meet them at the court in a few minutes. First I had to finish cooking my grandmother's dinner. They laughed and laughed.

"John, you're crazy," they teased. "You don't know how to cook. You're just scared to come out because you know it's over for you once you step onto the court."

I tried to convince them I could cook, but they didn't believe me. So I decided to give them a taste of the Master Chef's work. I reached in the oven, pulled out two of the smothered meatballs simmering in gravy and cut them in half so they could share.

"Man! This is good! John, you really can cook," they said.

"Yeah, I know. Now get out!" I replied.

I finished my grandmother's meal by making her a fresh pitcher of Brisk iced tea, her favorite, then prepared her plate and carried it to her room. While I helped her with her napkin, she looked up at me with her beautiful brown eyes.

"You're such a good grandson. Come and give an old lady a kiss." I kissed my granny on her forehead, ran into my room and threw on my shoes. Then I grabbed my basketball and headed for the court.

On my way down the driveway, I remembered that I had forgotten to give her the iced tea. I ran back up the driveway and inside, poured a glass of ice tea and went into Granny's room, but instead of contentedly enjoying her meal as I expected, I found her lying unresponsive on the floor.

The ambulance and my dad arrived almost simultaneously. The paramedics put my grandmother on the gurney and wheeled her to the ambulance. My dad and I jumped in his car and anxiously followed the ambulance to the hospital.

I had already prayed to God several times to make my grandmother better again. I asked Him to save her and to restore her strength, so she could return home safely. That's what they taught us in church. If you pray to God and ask for His help, He will help you, because God loves everyone.

At the hospital, I broke down. In the middle of the waiting room, I began screaming and crying like a hungry newborn baby. My dad rushed over and put his arms around me. "Everything is going to be okay. She's going to be fine, I guarantee you!" He said.

After a long three hours of waiting, a doctor came out to give my dad an update on my grandmother's condition. I began to pray again, "God, I'm begging you, please make my grandmother well again." But when my dad's head dropped, I knew she had passed away behind those large glass doors. At that moment, right there in the hospital, I cursed God, my church, and my overdressed pastor. I vowed never to pray or step foot into another church again as long as I lived.

That night, as I sat motionless on the edge of my bed, I tried to imagine what life was going to be like without my best friend, my sweetheart and the most important person in the world. The next morning my dad sat me down and talked for a long time about how life goes on after death. He tried to explain to me that my granny was in a better place. He actually did a pretty good job, but I wasn't paying attention. The only sound I could hear was my grandmother's voice playing in my head over and over and over, *John-John, did you brush your teeth? John-John, did you wash up?, John-John, did you use soap? John-John, are your pants pulled all the way up? John-John, do you have on clean underwear?* That night before I closed my eyes to go to sleep, I pictured my granny flying over the city on a beautiful white cloud. She was wearing her best Sunday dress and she was absolutely beautiful.

CHAPTER 5

When the *Love* is
GONE

"Tears are the words that the heart can't express."

-ANON

At age 14, all of the love in my heart was gone. My love for life, my love for school, my love for God, and my love for myself —all vanished. Still mourning my grandmother's death, and intimidated by my middle school teacher's speeches about high school and its rigorous demands, I entered one of the largest, most academically challenging high schools in my city. My fear was stuck to me like a helmet to a running back. I went from a middle school with three floors, 35 teachers, one gym, and 600 students to a school with eight floors, well over 150 teachers, a student body of 2,000, three gyms, and a cafeteria the size of a convention center.

I was unprepared for this tremendous transition. The pressure to excel, to adapt, and to acclimate proved overwhelming for me. I had six classes, basketball practice and chores at home, plus I now worked 30 hours a week at Bob & Don's Meat Market. I felt like a little paddleboat being tossed to and fro in the chaotic ocean of peer pressure and tumultuous emotions. I was unable to focus and, more importantly, I didn't have anyone to go to for help. Normally I would have gone to my dad, but we didn't see each other much, and I felt distant from him. Instead of attending classes, I hung out with upper classmen who were professional truants and naively depended on them to guide me. When I did decide to attend class, it wasn't because I wanted to get an education; it was because all of the classes were packed with beautiful girls who needed a "big daddy" in their life. (So I thought!)

At the conclusion of the first semester, my counselor called me down to her office. "Jonathan, your grades are very poor at this point," she said. "You received a 1.7 and a 1.5 on your first two report cards and that's unacceptable here. If your grades don't improve, you may be asked to leave. Therefore, from this point on, Mr. Edison, you will be placed on academic probation."

I left her office with my heart in my stomach. I had never been on academic probation, or any type of probation for that matter, in my life. I had always considered myself to be a smart kid, so how could I suddenly be doing so terribly now? I became even more focused on trying to blend in and hide the fact that I was struggling. My grades got even worse.

By the third card marking, my confidence, self-esteem, and hunger for knowledge had evaporated. My grade point average was a whopping 1.4. I started to believe that I was a dumb, good-for-nothing kid who didn't deserve to attend Cass Technical High School.

At the end of the second semester, I was called to the office and handed a manila envelope. There was a letter inside.

To the parents of Jonathan Edison:
Due to poor academic performance and low achievement, your son/daughter will not be allowed to return to Cass Technical High School in the fall of 1988. It is apparent that the rigors of such a demanding environment are too much for him/her to handle right now. So, it is with deep regret that we must inform you that your son/daughter has been academically dismissed. Remember he/she is no longer a Cass Technical High School student and should not

return to the school grounds. He/she is to report to his neighborhood high school to continue his/her education.

I felt like the biggest failure on the planet. That's when I decided to drop out of school altogether. That summer my mind was in turmoil. I became heedless and reckless. I stayed out all times of the night, walking the streets and wondering what life was going to throw at me next. With the burden of being kicked out of school on my mind and my grandmother's death seared into my psyche, my thoughts were now my own worst enemy. As I looked for someone to sympathize with my plight, I turned to Jerome Bailey.

He was 16, stood six feet, eight inches tall, lived on the same block and had already dropped out of high school because his basketball coach didn't select him for the team in ninth grade. He was so devastated that he gave up going to school and stayed home, drowning his sorrows in malt liquor and marijuana. He was the perfect role model. (NOT!) I found myself sitting in his living room watching him smoke marijuana and drink beer. After a few sips of Old English Malt Liquor and a couple whiffs of second-hand marijuana smoke, I discovered beer and weed made me violently ill. I tried to do it but my body wouldn't allow me. (Thank God.)

In late July, my dad sold our house. He moved into a three-bedroom apartment so I could have my own room. We packed all of my belongings and I moved in with my new family: Tanzella, Starmaine and Demetrius. Unsurprisingly, the hostility was instantaneous. I was accustomed to coming and going as I pleased and doing what I wanted, when I wanted. In my mind, I was a grown man and deserved to be treated like one. But my stepmother didn't see it that way. She wanted me to follow her rules and her rules only. That meant no cooking in the house after 8:00 p.m., no visitors of any kind, no leaving the house after 9:00 p.m., no staying up past 11:00 p.m., and definitely no wrestling moves on her couch or in her living room. Her number one rule, which she constantly reminded me of, was to put the toilet seat back down after I used the bathroom. She was so obsessed with that damn toilet seat rule that she made a bright red sign especially for me and taped it to my bedroom door: "Make sure you put the toilet seat down!!"

My father took her side on every issue concerning me. He would come home from work most nights and give me a speech about how I made her unhappy and feel bad by disrespecting her rules. I ate too much, I made too much noise, I showered too long, I left the toilet seat up, I slammed the door too hard, I didn't talk to my sister enough, I couldn't be trusted, I made her nervous, I talked too much, I laughed too loud. I felt like my father had turned against me. After the third week of living with them, I had enough.

One night I stayed out until 12:30 a.m. When I returned to the apartment, she was waiting for me. As soon as I walked through the door, she started screaming about how stupid I was and how I didn't listen and how she wished I had never been born. Fed up! I gave her a piece of my mind. *"Lady, you're crazy, you're a real nut job and you're not my mother so stop telling me what to do! You get on my freaking nerves and I hate you!"* I yelled at her. The next morning, I told my dad what had happened. "Boy, don't you ever talk to my wife like that again as long as you live," he bellowed. "You better get your act together before I send you to juvenile."

"You don't have to send me anywhere, I'll leave on my own," I fired back. "You don't want me here anyway!"

My father stood up with his fists in gear. "When are you leaving?"

"Right now," I yelled.

I ran up to my room, grabbed my book bag, my suitcase, and my life savings of $300 and stormed out of the apartment. I didn't know where I was going. I walked and walked and walked for hours. By the time I realized where I was, I had walked all the way to my old high school, nearly 6 miles away from my dad's house. At sundown, I found myself in Cass Corridor, an area of Detroit plagued with drugs, prostitution, homelessness, and sleazy one-hour motels.

As I approached the corner of Cass Boulevard and Woodward, I had flashbacks of my childhood, walking to the food stamp office with my mother. I was tired, hungry, hurt, disgusted, and fed up with my father and his wife. How could he choose that woman over me? I was his son.

I walked up to the counter of one of the one-hour motels and checked in. I paid $18 for the night, got my key, and headed for the room. It was the "second" vilest place on earth. The smell of urine greeted me when I opened the door. The room was dark and filthy. There was no running water and no room service. The bed was a bare twin sized mattress sitting on a cot in the middle of the floor and held the history of thousands of sex acts. At least the lamp worked so I could keep an eye on the roaches trying to climb into my suitcase. My stomach growled, but I was afraid of being robbed or attacked if I went to a store, so I just sat there trying to stay awake.

The next morning a loud banging on the door woke me up.

"Hey, boy! Either pay now for another night or get out!"

I paid a week in advance, hoping an angel would rescue me. On the sixth night, I was on my way to the party store on the corner when a longtime friend of my mother's saw me walking and stopped me.

"John-John, is that you?" Mary cried. "Come here, son! What in the world are you doing here in Cass Corridor? Are you crazy? Don't you know what type of neighborhood you're in?"

With tears running down my face, I screamed frantically without warning, "Mary, I have run away from my father's house, my grandmother is dead, and I don't know where my mother is!! Can you please help me?" The shock registered immediately on Mary's face. Her smile faded and grief, compassion, and horror played across her features as she listened. Then she pulled me close, gave me a big bear hug and whispered everything was going to be ok.

Mary drove me to my aunt Elizabeth's house, my mother's sister, a nurse who lived near Detroit City Airport. My aunt Elizabeth was sympathetic to my situation as Mary explained to her what was going on. Thankfully, my aunt kindly agreed to allow me to live there if I promised to clean up after myself and pay her $50 a month in rent and half of the light bill, so of course I agreed.

I worked up enough courage to call my father and made arrangements to get the rest of my things several weeks later. My cousin Jamall owned a pickup and volunteered to help by giving me a lift to my dad's, but when we arrived, my dad made it perfectly clear that the only things that belonged to me were the clothes on my back.

"You're not taking anything out of this house. You can have the box spring and that's it." My father yelled.

Jamall and I hauled the box spring outside to the truck. The entire time my dad never said a word. He waited for me to clear the threshold of the front door and then he slammed the door and locked it behind me.

CHAPTER 6

DEJA VU/
Can it Get Any *Worse?*

"God thought something was so interesting; that he had to rewind it to show all of his friends."

-ANONYMOUS

Aunt Elizabeth's house wasn't in the greatest condition. The living room smelled like a high school football locker room. The carpet was covered in dirt, dog hair and was also infested with fleas. The upstairs bathroom was small with a broken sink that only produced lukewarm water. The shower and tub were virtually impossible to use because of the mold, fungus, and mildew that was growing on the floor of the tub. The kitchen was a train wreck with an empty refrigerator, dirty dishes for days and trash that was overflowing out of the trash can. I was given direction by my aunt to set up camp in the basement next to the furnace. When I first walked down the stairs I immediately covered my nose because of the putrid smell that rushed into my nostrils. I soon realized that this smell was created by years of neglect, rotting pipes, and frequent semi-floods that took place in the basement. My aunt alerted to the fact that every time someone washed their clothes or flushed the upstairs toilet the drain could possibly back up and overflow. With this pertinent information, I decided to place my box spring on four milk crates. I also propped up a huge black footlocker trunk where I kept all of my clothes and personal belongings. I didn't have a television or radio, but the dripping water from the sweating pipes and the hum of the furnace provided enough background noise to satisfy my need for rhythm and beats. I got a job at Chili's Grill & Bar washing dishes and bussing tables, earning $5.25 an hour for the dishes and $2.51 an hour for the bussing.

I didn't really know if I wanted to go back to school or not, but my aunt convinced me to give high school another try. She persuaded me to register at Osborn High School. Osborn was a rough place to learn compared to Cass. Cass Technical High School was filled with kids who had bright futures and big dreams of college and beyond. Most Cass Tech students came from affluent, two-parent households that held education in high regard. Cass students were also uniquely different because they had to test in to be accepted, and the curriculum was rigorous. In comparison, Osborn High School was run more like a detention center. At the entrance to the school stood six or seven oversized security guards, all armed with Mace, flashlights, handcuffs, and metal body wands. The hallway floors were covered in balled-up paper, potato chip wrappers, and soda cans. The teachers looked tired and worn down. Osborn struggled with gang activity, violence, and high dropout and pregnancy rates. Some Osborn students who lived on my block filled my head with horror stories of what went on inside Osborn. They described the gangs, the violence, the drugs, and the lack of attentiveness by the teachers.

I was nervous but I thought if the school had all those things going on, the chaos would easily take the focus off me and how dumb I was. I felt it would be much easier to fit in and go unnoticed. Even after the advance warning, I could not believe the mayhem that existed inside the school—kids fought in the hallways, kicked over vending machines, openly sold drugs, and even beat up teachers.

I did my best to steer clear of the violence. I wasn't a bad kid, but I wasn't exceptionally bright either. I didn't have all Fs, but I didn't have all As, and was more worried about saving money to buy another pair of Air Jordan's than about my grades. I was quiet and reserved, a prime candidate for falling through the cracks. I did go to class most of the time, but it wasn't to get an education. It was to see how many girls showed up that day. I had no leadership, focus, or direction for my life. My aunt did the best she could with me but her primary concern was the $50 on the first of the month and half of the light bill. She even charged a $5-a-day late fee if I didn't pay on time.

I had not spoken with my father since the day I left the house with my mattress.

Since I didn't start work until 5:00 p.m., I needed something to fill my afternoons. The only thing that lit my fire and got me excited was sports. Playing basketball was the one thing that I could do extremely well. I would have tried out for the team, but my grades were too low. But in my backyard, I was king. I practiced for hours after school, on the weekends and in the dark. It was addictive, but it was a form of release and an escape from reality. In my backyard everything was perfect when it came to basketball.

It was one of the only places where I was in complete control, dominated everyone, and no one could stop me. But outside my backyard, I was a nobody with no power, no pride, and going nowhere fast.

I had my first meeting with my guidance counselor, Mrs. Davis, at the beginning of my senior year. She told me that if I attended night school and made up an English class I had flunked the previous year, I could graduate, even with all Ds. I realized that a diploma meant I could attend college, and maybe make it to the NBA. I paid the $59 fee and enrolled. I passed the English class with a D, which joined two other Ds and a C on my final report card. I graduated from Osborn High School with an overall grade point average of 1.62. I was ranked 328th out of a class of 420.

I was excited about the idea of going to college until I started reading the requirements. "All students must have a minimum GPA of 2.0. All students must take the SAT and/or the ACT and achieve a midlevel score. All students must have three letters of recommendation." I met none of the requirements. After four years of high school, I had a piece of paper that said "diploma" on it, but it was worthless. I couldn't write a paragraph, I finished all my math classes with Ds or Fs, and I was reading on an 8th grade level. Three short years at Osborn High School had turned me into a complete idiot. The only good thing that came out of my high school diploma was the graduation ceremony, and that's because my father came. I couldn't believe that he actually showed up. I was definitely shocked because since I had left the house we had only seen each other a few times. During my senior year though, he actually popped in on me for a couple of surprise visits. His visits were always unannounced and they were very brief. He would always ask if I needed anything and how my life was progressing. Around May of that year, he made one of his surprise visits, and I decided to give him one of my five invitations to the graduation ceremony.

Graduation day was a good day, a day of victory, a day of joy, and a day of accomplishment. After the ceremony, my father met me outside and told me that he was proud of me. He said if I ever needed his help, I could call him. Then he reached in his pocket and pulled out a $50 bill. He handed it to me and said:

"Good luck. Now I have to go back to work."

After he left, I walked over to the parking lot and sat down, still in my cap and gown. I thought of my grandmother, looked up to the sky, and began talking to her.

"Granny, look at your grandson now. I hope you're proud of me. I know my grades weren't the best but I promise you, I will make something out of myself. I love you."

CHAPTER 7

But *You* PROMISED

"Promises are like babies: easy to make, hard to deliver."

-JONATHAN EDISON

I set a goal for myself: I was going to use my athletic ability to get out of my aunt's basement and into the penthouse of life. After graduation, I started practicing day and night, hoping to land a tryout opportunity at any college that would accept me. My cousin PJ, a couple of our drug dealer buddies, and my new best friend, Melvin Cokley, decided to enter into a 5-on-5 tournament that a lot of college scouts would be visiting. We actually did fairly well, considering the stiff competition, which was much more organized. We finished fourth. When our games were over, we decided to hang around the tournament and watch the championship games still in progress. That's when I met Coach J, a recruiter from Fort Valley State College in Fort Valley, Georgia. He pulled me to the side.

"Son, has anyone ever told you that you got game? How would you like the opportunity to come down to my college and play ball for me?"

My mouth went dry. I swallowed but didn't say anything. Melvin popped me in the back of my head. "John, say something, bro. Are you deaf? Answer the man."

"Where do I sign up?" I asked. "What do I need to do?" Then I remembered my grades. "Uhhhhhhhhhhhhh, Coach J, I really appreciate your offer and everything, but I think you should know that uhhhhhhhhhh, my GPA is only 1.6," I mumbled, dropping my head.

"Son, that doesn't matter. We take care of our own at Fort Valley

State," he said. "All you have to do is get there, and you got it!" Then he winked at me, revealing a gold tooth. Bling! "Meet me on campus on September 5 and I'll take care of everything else. Son, I promise you, you're going to have the time of your life. Free room and board, free food and a full athletic scholarship, and more importantly, you will be playing basketball for a great college. See ya in September."

I decided to take my dad up on his offer to help. I called him and rattled off everything the coach had told me. Of course, my dad being my dad, he wanted to have a long drawn-out conversation about my big decision.

"Son, don't you think that you should spend some time thinking about this?" he asked. "Where's the paperwork? Who is this guy? Do you have a brochure? How do you know this is the real deal?" My father peppered me with question after question after question, blah, blah, blah. For the most part, I tuned him out.

"Pops, come on, he promised. This is my one big chance. You said if I needed your help, you would be here to help me. So are you going to help me or not?"

Finally he realized that I was serious and determined to fulfill my dream, so he agreed to assist me. He paid for my plane ticket and drove me to the airport. This was it, my big moment. At last I was leaving the nest and traveling 800 miles to pursue my dream. I shook my dad's hand and walked over toward the gate. I gave the attendant my boarding pass, and just before I walked through the tunnel, I turned around. I looked my dad square in the eyes and said, "Daddy, don't worry. I'm a man. I GOT THIS!"

I will never forget the look in my father's eyes and his nod when I said that to him. On the exterior, it may seem like a simple gesture, but beneath the surface and in the realm of the soul, a nod from a father to son is an acknowledgement of effort, confidence, and most importantly, love. At least, that's the way it always felt for us.

When I arrived at the college, I saw about 500 students waiting to register. I headed straight for the front of the line. After all, superstars don't wait in line like common folk.

"Excuse me, Miss," I said. "I'm sure you've already heard about me, so please tell me where my room is."

"Son, I don't know who you are," she replied. "Now tell me who sent you down here?"

"Coach J sent me. He said that I'm the Man."

She gave me a strange look and started to check the names on the list. Then suddenly she stopped. "Did you say Coach J, as in Johnson?"

"Yes, that's the one." I said.

"I see the problem now. Son, Coach J was fired last week. You didn't know that? Oh well, sorry. Now get out of my line. Next!"

"What the heck do you mean he was fired?" I hollered.

"Somebody better hire him back right now!"

Campus security police showed up and escorted me to the president's office where I was forced to explain my situation to the president. He was unsympathetic to my plight. Instead, he advised me to return home and to consider trying again next year. But I couldn't. I would not go back home a failure. So I got a job working at McDonald's and bounced around from dorm to dorm. It was amazing, because everyone was very sympathetic to my plight. It turns out it's very easy to find friendly people that are willing to take you in for days at a time, especially if they are from your part of the country. So for weeks I would stay with what we called "homeboys" because they were from Detroit. And I met quite a few nice guys from the Miami area that loved to party. So after parties, I would hang out and crash with them for a few days.

Luckily for me, my cousin Shaniqua was already a student at Fort Valley State, and she introduced me to her good friend David Eakins, a star player on the basketball team. When I met David, he shared an off campus apartment with his girlfriend Dee Dee and one other guy from the basketball team. They had a spare bedroom they let me sleep in for $150 a month. I also applied for financial aid and emergency funds that the college occasionally released.

After months of working at McDonald's and waiting for my financial aid to clear, I was finally able to attend class like a regular student. There was only one hitch: because my high school grades were so poor, my advisor recommended that I register for college refresher courses. As soon as I heard that, it was like my heart curled up and died. I sank into a deep depression. It was official—I was a cross-country idiot, successfully stupid in not only one state but two. Dejectedly, I registered for the suggested remedial classes but my heart wasn't in it. My self-esteem was shot, and my inner man had suffered a knockout blow. I had no more interest in sports or living in the extremely hot state of Georgia. Given my academic performance, I was ineligible anyway, and would be for at least a year until I pulled my grades up. I was extremely impatient at that age, and I wasn't willing to wait that long. If an opportunity didn't present itself to me immediately, I found something else.

I tried to persevere. I stayed in classes for another semester before I decided enough was enough. I officially dropped out of Fort Valley State College in the spring of 1992, finishing my career with a cumulative average of 0.82.

CHAPTER 8

A *Wake-up* CALL

"Determination is the wake-up call to the human will."

-ANTHONY ROBBINS

The 36-hour Greyhound bus ride back to Detroit gave me ample time to reflect back on my life. I thought about my grandmother's love and positive influence, and the promise I had made to her to make something of myself. I thought about the afternoon that I left home and how I confidently told my dad I was a man. He was going to be so disappointed in me. I reminisced about how great my middle school days were, and I remembered my mother sleeping in that old rundown warehouse. I thought about the day at the park when Coach J promised to give me a full scholarship if I came to Georgia, and although I am sure no one could tell by looking at me, I even thought about completely giving up on life.

The negative thoughts started to take over. I felt as if I, the son of a drug-addicted mother and a college dropout, had nothing else to live for. My assessment of my life shaped up like this: I had barely graduated high school; I was an outcast from my father's house; I was a failure in the eyes of many, including myself. I was selfish, self-centered, full of pride, bad tempered, poor, and black. I had cursed God out of my life. My future was bleak, and the only thing left to do was give my life over to the devil, or so I thought.

I took a cab to my aunt's house from the Greyhound bus terminal. It turned out the taxicab driver was also a part-time youth pastor at a church in downtown Detroit. He opened up the conversation by asking me where I was going and where I was coming from. I told him my long pity party story about how I had left for school and things didn't work out, and about how I was feeling like a complete failure. He didn't interrupt me, he just listened. When I stopped talking to take a breath he asked very quietly, "Do you know that your heavenly Father loves you?"

"What?" I replied.

"Yes. Do you know that your heavenly Father loves you?" he repeated.

"What does that have to do with anything?" I asked.

"God never gives you more than you can handle. God was just testing you, attempting to buffet your flesh for your future. First Corinthians 9:27."

"Buffet my flesh for my future?" I asked. This guy wasn't making any sense.

"Yes! You see, if God has big plans for you in the future, He gives you challenges in the present that get you prepared for your future. 'I buffet my body and subdue it, for fear that after proclaiming to others the Gospel and things pertaining to it, I myself should become unfit.'"

"Ahhh. So what you're saying is that everything that happened to me was for a reason beyond my comprehension."

"Yes, and trust me . . . you are going to do something great one day!"

He witnessed to me about the goodness of God and spoke to that dead part of my spirit. Then right there in his cab, he prayed the Prayer of Salvation over me and suddenly, I let out a roar deep from my soul. I don't know what happened, except after that encounter, I felt God return to my heart. I felt like living once again, as if I was recharged and infused with new energy. I believe the Angel of God spoke to me in the form of that taxi driver.

The next day, I called Chili's Grill & Bar and begged for my old job back. Carlos, the manager that was responsible for my training, rehired me. I was ready to wash dishes, play basketball and live in my aunt's basement, for the rest of my life. I had a routine again that gave me what I wanted…a sense of stability and a sense of purpose, even if I was just doing the same thing as before I left Detroit.

About a month after I moved back to Detroit, PJ, Melvin, and I were having one of our knockdown, drag-out, ball-until-you-fall basketball tournaments in the backyard with the usual cast of shady characters, who played 3-on-3 basketball with enough jewelry on them to make Liberace blush. Melvin and I were in a zone and couldn't be beat or stopped, and no matter what team they put on the floor against us, we disposed of them. It was my backyard and I was on top of my game. Not only did we dominate the other teams with our play, we brutalized them with our trash talking. I talked so much trash I could have started a riot. Then one of the thugs decided that he had heard enough from me. He snatched the ball out of my hands and threw it over the fence.

"You big dumb fool, you need to go back to school," I taunted him. "Boy, don't you know we can't be beat. Wait, stop! I think I smell your feet. Let me tell you something, Bo Bo, throwing the king's ball is a no-no. You better not let it happen again, or you're going to meet my little friend."

Everyone laughed. I jumped the fence, retrieved the ball, returned to the yard, and started shooting around by myself. Then the laughter stopped. The backyard went deathly silent. I turned around to see what was going on and the serial criminal Ike Lathem was standing a mere three feet away from me holding a loaded .357 Magnum pointed directly at my head. As I held that basketball in my hand, I mumbled, "Please don't kill me. I don't want to die. Please don't kill me."

He pulled the trigger. BLAM! But PJ's friend Marvin hit Ike's arm just as he pulled the trigger, and thanks to him, the bullet whizzed inches above my head and hit the garage door behind me. I had never been shot at before and that was definitely the most scared I've ever been in my life.

Thank you for saving my life, Marvin. You are truly an angel from God. May God bless you and your family with a long, healthy and abundant life.

JONATHAN EDISON

CHAPTER 9

Rumble, Young Man,
RUMBLE

"Don't count the days, make the days count."

-MUHAMMAD ALI

Following that incident, I changed my entire focus as I remembered the promise I had made to my grandmother on the day of my graduation from high school. I was determined to keep my promise, as well as to prove my teacher wrong. Because even though she believed that I was going to turn out to be a failure or addicted to drugs. I didn't have to allow her opinion to become my reality!

That summer my life began to turn for the better. While at the mall having lunch with a few friends, I met a beautiful young lady named Carla Stamps who was out shopping with her mother. Carla was incredibly beautiful, smart, and she was a 1991 University of Michigan graduate. Although she was a few years older than I, that didn't seem to matter after we spent the summer getting to know each other. We went out on many fun dates, to the movies, dinner, summer festivals in Detroit and surprisingly, art fairs. I wasn't big into art, but she managed to open my eyes and pique my interest. She also took me to several U of M alumni events that were filled with "upper class" educated folks who were cultured and sophisticated. This was a far cry from the set of friends that I was used to. The most we ever did was play basketball in my backyard and go to an occasional movie. I had never been to an art gallery, or congregated with friends who were able to engage in insightful and intelligent conversation about politics and current events.

Carla was a breath of fresh air in my life that summer. She was cultured, refined, educated, and open to sharing her experiences with me to make me a more well-rounded person. Visiting her family on special occasions was a highlight for me. Carla's family was like a real-life version of the Cosby Show. Carla's father Roland was a fire chief for the Detroit Fire Department. Carla's mother was an attorney, her little brother Roland Jr. and little sister Rosalyn were both honor roll students in high school, and Rosalyn was even part of all-girls band. If this wasn't the Huxtables live and in living color, I don't know what was.

After spending the summer together, Carla began to ask me about my future and what I had planned. One Saturday we went out for a late dinner at the local Elias Brothers/Big Boy Restaurant. She went into her purse and pulled out a couple of napkins. On one napkin she wrote **Short Term Goals,** and on the other napkin she wrote **Long Term Goals.**

"Jonathan, I want to teach you how to plan for your future. It's a technique that my father taught all of us many years ago, and it has worked for me my entire life. I think it could help you too. Have you ever actually thought about and written down your goals?"

"No, I haven't...I've thought about things that I want to accomplish, but I can't say that I have ever written down anything...does it really matter if I write them down or not?"

"Oh, yes! When you write your goals down, that makes them real in your imagination and mind. Then after you write them down you can revisit them as often as you like to see if you're on course or if you have gotten off track. So, my dear, what are your goals?"

"What are my goals?" I asked inquisitively.

"Yes, what are your goals? We can deal with the Short Term goals first."

"Short Term? What exactly does that mean?"

"Ok, like, between three months and a year. What would you like to accomplish?"

"Between three months and a year...Hmmm, that's a good question. How about a kiss to spark my imagination?"

"Boy! I'm serious! What would you like to accomplish three months to a year from now?"

As we sat there at 1 a.m. in the Elias Brothers/Big Boy dining room, she began to press me for answers. She didn't let me off the hook with my usual side stepping and avoiding hard questions with semi-funny jokes.

"Jonathan, you have to get serious about your life. You can't live in your aunt's basement and work at Chili's until you die. C'mon, baby, think, what do you want to do three months to a year from now?"

I sat there and stared out of the window and then it hit me.

"I want to go back to college within the next three months to a year."

"Wow, that's awesome. What college?"

"I don't know, any college, especially any college that will accept my grades. I didn't tell you this before, but they were really low coming out of high school and then during my stint at Fort Valley State College."

She wasn't fazed, and she didn't ask me how low. I think she could tell I was a little embarrassed. She just said, "You know, you can take remedial classes at the local Community College to get your education back on track."

She went on to explain that remedial classes at Wayne County Community College were very inexpensive and they were designed especially for students like me that needed an extra boost and academic support. I immediately got excited. What Carla was explaining gave me hope! So I took the pen she offered, and I wrote down on the top of the Short Term Goals napkin: Enroll in remedial classes at Wayne County Community College.

For the rest of the weekend, all I could think about was the possibility of going back to college. That Monday morning before I went to work, I took the bus up to Wayne County Community College. When I arrived on the campus I was anxious to see what the possibilities were. Right as I was getting off the bus, I reached into my front pocket and pulled out that napkin with my Short Term Goals. At the top of the list, and as a matter of fact, the only goal on that napkin was registering at Wayne County Community College. I made my way to the registrar's office, and they quickly confirmed I was not eligible to attend regular classes and would definitely have to go the remedial route. I knew that going in, but it was still very embarrassing to have someone tell me to my face. It pretty much highlighted the fact that I was a failure, and to be quite honest, after walking out of the registrar's office, I felt horrible! But I tried to locate the office where the remedial class registration was being held. When I walked in, I caught the eye of a woman who not only changed my perspective, but the trajectory of my entire educational life.

Her name was Ms. Betty Coates. She was a short African -American woman with a bit of a Geri curl, a gold tooth and a southern accent. She was also the new program director and recruiter for the Urban Teachers Program implemented that year at Wayne County Community College. We struck up a conversation and she asked why I had the long face. I started to explain how I did not meet the criteria for normal registration, but she stopped me in my tracks and asked me if I would consider taking a few remedial classes. I looked up at her, smiled, and I pulled out my neatly folded napkin and showed her the top of my list.

"Wow, Jonathan, it looks like we're on the same page."

"Yes, ma'am, it sure does."

By fall of 1993, I accomplished my first short-term goal. I successfully registered for remedial classes at Wayne County Community College.

Surprisingly, my instructors were really encouraging and great at providing the extra support I needed to get up to speed. Who would have guessed after one year, I would be on the brink of taking "real" courses at the college, because I had passed the remedial ones with flying colors? Ms. Coates was so excited, happy, and proud of me. She said she always knew I had it in me to get it done. I think Ms. Coates was sent directly from heaven. She was always there for me, helping me navigate classes and balance out my hectic schedule.

The semester I began taking actual classes, I worked full time at Chili's for 50 hours a week and was attempting 25 credits. It was a crazy and amazingly hectic existence, because all I did was eat, sleep, work, and study for the next year. However, all of my hard work paid off. I learned if I completed one more year, I could graduate with an associate's degree and start a career in the Detroit public school system as an educational technician, earning $18 an hour. With this newfound information, I mentally put the pedal to the metal and started breezing through classes. Unfortunately, and right in the middle of the semester, I lost my job at Chili's because of a scheduling conflict. My manager wanted me to slow down on the classes and work more hours at the restaurant, but I decided my education was more important than washing dishes. I was doing great in class, but I still needed to make money to cover my living expenses.

Fortunately, I got the opportunity to take a job as a bus attendant. The bus attendant gig was great because I worked a split shift, three hours in the morning and less than two hours in the afternoon. I could continue to take classes in the middle of the day, and also pick up a second gig at the local Mobile gas station. That job was three days a week on the graveyard shift, 11 p.m.–6 a.m. Now my schedule was really out of control.

SEE SCHEDULE BELOW:

SUNDAY

MOBILE GAS STATION	11:00pm – 6:00am
STUDY TIME	

MONDAY

BUS TERMINAL	6:30am – 9:30am
CLASS 1	11:00am – 12:00pm
CLASS 3	12:00pm – 2:00pm
BUS TERMINAL	3:00pm – 4:30pm
CLASS 5	5:30pm – 7:30pm

TUESDAY

BUS TERMINAL	6:30am – 9:30am
CLASS 2	1:00pm – 2:30pm
BUS TERMINAL	3:00pm – 4:30pm
CLASS 5	6:00pm – 8:00pm

WEDNESDAY

Bus Terminal	6:30am – 9:30am
Class 1	11:00am – 12:00pm
Class 3	12:00pm – 2:00pm
Bus Terminal	3:00pm – 4:30pm
Class 5	5:30pm – 7:30pm

THURSDAY

Bus Terminal	6:30am – 9:30am
Class 2	1:00pm – 2:30pm
Bus Terminal	3:00pm – 4:30pm
Class 5	6:00pm – 8:00pm

FRIDAY

Bus Terminal	6:30am – 9:30am
Class 1	11:00am – 12:00pm
Class 3	12:00pm – 2:00pm
Bus Terminal	3:00pm – 4:30pm
Mobile Gas Station	11:00pm – 6:00am

SATURDAY

Mobile Gas Station	11:00pm – 6:00am
Study Time	
Class 4	11:00am – 2:00pm
Study Time	

The only thing missing was having my own place, and for the last year I was working towards my degree, I was finally able to secure my own apartment. Cadillac Towers, located in downtown Detroit, was offering a $299 student studio apartment special with HBO and all utilities included—Hallelujah!

The place was so small I could flush the toilet, make breakfast, change the TV channel and look through the peephole all at the same time, but it was mine. I will never forget that day, it was a bright and sunny Tuesday afternoon when I moved in. I stopped at the local Chinese restaurant for a #2 Feast, went over to the rental office, and picked up my keys.

In my neighborhood, if you could afford Chinese takeout during the week, you were doing pretty well. That night I sat on the floor of the living room/bedroom/family room/workout room of my new studio apartment, ate my Chinese food with tears of joy welling up in my eyes. In that moment, sitting on the floor with my #2 Feast, I was so happy. I wish I could have bottled that MOMENT and saved some of it for later.

I was finally my own man, with my own place and my own sense of purpose. No more basement floors and garbage bag suitcases for me. I vowed on the day I moved in I would never live in another basement as long as I lived.

Shortly before I was due to graduate, I stopped in on Ms. Coates to catch up and to share my progress with her. Naturally she wanted to know what my future plans were. Future plans?

"Yes, Jonathan," I recall her inquiring, "what are your future plans beyond graduation? Are you going to pursue your four-year degree at a university?"

I actually never even entertained the idea of moving on to the next level, but she was able to help me see a larger vision of myself. She helped me see beyond Community College and into the future where she knew that I would thrive. So during my final two semesters at Wayne County Community College I registered for classes at Wayne State University in the evening and on Saturday. *(You weren't supposed to do that but I was on a mission…shhhhhhh)* Between both the community college and the university, I was registered for a total of 34 credits—I knew it was a risk, but I was excited about my education again, and I felt unstoppable. In May of 1995, I completed my Associates Degree in the Urban Teachers Program from Wayne County Community College, and in December of 1996, I completed my Bachelor of Science degree from Wayne State University. But I still had a major obstacle keeping me from my goal of becoming a classroom teacher. Dun, dun, dun…. the Michigan Teacher Certification Test. In order to become a fully licensed teacher, you had to pass the test, and I had heard it was a doozie.

I started studying for the test about a year and a half before graduation. On my first attempt, I did pretty well, but came up a few points short on the social studies section. I didn't give it a second thought; I just registered for the next exam date, knowing I had plenty of time to complete this requirement. I took the test again, only this time, I didn't pass the science section. I was livid. I had studied, I knew the material, and I made sure I took my time when answering the questions. What the heck? After the second failure, I decided to join a study group. We met twice a week to go over the material, and practice questions. After a month of studying like crazy people, we were all ready and pumped for the next date to take the exam. Early Saturday morning I took the test again, and this time I felt really confident. I was well rested, I knew the material, and I was focused. Well, none of that mattered, because when the results came in, I had failed for the third time. I was beside myself, but nevertheless, the one thing I knew was I couldn't give up. With each failure I dug in even harder. I was not going to allow a standardized test to get in the way of my goal of becoming a classroom teacher. When it was all said and done, I failed the Michigan Teacher Certification Test seven times before successfully passing it, but I passed it!

In the fall of 1997, I was hired as a classroom teacher at Spain Middle School, teaching 4th grade homeroom. That same year, I decided to become an entrepreneur and to open up my first business, Edison's Fitness, Inc. Private Personal Training Center. I had a few hours at the end of the day after school let out, and I knew I had to get another revenue stream going for the summer, when my teaching salary would go on hold. The plan was to find a way to make it through the summer without having to teach summer school and wait tables, like most of my colleagues did every year. Back then, and to this day, I had a passion for physical fitness and working out, so it made perfect sense for me to turn what I loved to do into a home-based business.

I only had three hundred dollars, but the lack of capital didn't stop me. I bought mirror squares from Home Depot, purchased a few dumbbells from K-Mart, and even borrowed an old mat from the middle school's gym to place on the floor. I even went as far as to create my business's sign at the Spain curriculum lab and had it laminated. I was ready to make it happen, only there was one tiny problem—I didn't have any clients or any marketing materials. *(This was pre-websites).* The Power House Gym and Vic Tanny dominated the market at the time. But in my mind, that was a small issue, because I've always known how to be innovative. I reviewed the structures for both of those rival businesses carefully, and realized their personal training fees were really expensive. Powerhouse Gym charged $25 a session and required a membership, while Vic Tanny cost $30 an hour, plus a recurring membership rate of $99.00 a month.

I decided to undercut their price by offering three 1-hour sessions for $40 and no membership fee. Who could resist having a personal trainer for only forty bucks? Now the question was, where was I going to get these new clients? Sitting in the salon one morning, waiting for my weekly haircut, it hit me. Hair salons! Women all across the city go to hair salons every Saturday morning, so I decided to make hair salons my stomping grounds for marketing my new business.

The first Saturday morning of the month I did 500 pushups, put on a tank top, and walked into the Directions Hair Salon in Downtown Detroit. I stood in the middle of the shop and shouted the magic question to over seventy women who were waiting to have their hair done:

"Who needs a personal trainer?" In a very deep and sexy voice!

Jackpot! Giving demonstrations right there in the middle of the salon, I picked up twenty new clients. Even though I taught during the day, I was able to have an extremely successful business. I took my first client at 5:00 a.m., left to teach school at 7, and then trained clients again from 4:00 p.m. until 10 p.m. Life was good. I was earning a solid salary teaching, and I was making great money personal training that year. Around the same time, I learned that Detroit Public Schools had just implemented a new policy, giving teachers who completed a Master's degree an automatic $5,000 raise. I didn't have to be told twice. I immediately enrolled in classes. Three semesters later, in December of 1998, I was awarded a Master's Degree of Education in Leadership and Supervision.

Business was booming, my career was taking off, and everything was perfect—until my nosy neighbor's butt got in the way. Like many neighborhoods, mine had a nosy resident who couldn't mind her own business. The lady directly across the lot from me, Mrs. Evelyn, complained about people constantly parking in her parking spot to the manager of our apartment complex. She also reported that she had witnessed dozens of women coming in and out my townhouse at all hours of the day and night. After a brief investigation, the rental office notified me under the terms of my lease, I could not operate a business out of my home, and I had to discontinue service immediately or face eviction. This was a crushing blow. I had to do something, and do something fast.

I decided to turn what seemed like lemons into lemonade. I immediately began looking for space for the new and improved Edison's Fitness, Inc. My new digs would include a juice bar, hot tub, shower and a low impact step class. I also began to look for a new place to live. After a few weeks of searching, I found the perfect place for both my gym and my new residence. The gym was in Ferndale, about ten miles north of downtown Detroit. The place needed a little work, but I cut a deal with the landlord to pay $400 a month up front for two years in return for handling the repairs myself. It took about an additional $6,000 to get the place to match just how I saw in my vision: new paint, new mirrors, new carpet, updated equipment, new showers, juice bar, Wall of Fame, and of course Edison's Fitness T-shirts. We were up and rolling after just 45 days of planning and construction.

Meanwhile, I signed a lease for my new residence in the prestigious Harbortown Apartments and Condominiums. Behind the highly secured gates of the Harbortown entrance was where Detroit's elite resided: millionaires, doctors, lawyers, business owners, land developers, musicians, politicians—the list went on. My Spinnaker Lane apartment overlooked the Detroit River into Canada. At age 25, just like George and Weeezie, I was moving on up to a deluxe apartment in the sky.

But as the year went on business became increasingly tough. My old clients didn't like my new location. It wasn't convenient to drive to, and didn't have the same quaint feel as my old place. By month three in the new space, my clientele had dropped over

85 percent. I struggled to keep the place afloat, and my only saving grace was the fact I had paid the lease up in advance. For the next six months, the basics like insurance, phone, water, gas, electric, and payroll came straight out of my teaching salary. I didn't know what to do to get the gym back on track. I tried everything: two for one specials, free smoothies, cookouts, but nothing worked. I even increased the hours the gym was open. As Edison's Fitness continued to spiral downward, I put together a backup plan to go back to school and complete my Ph.D. At the end of the year I enrolled into the Educational Specialist program at Wayne State University, which was the first step to completing the Ph.D. program. I remember leaving class to go up to Edison's Fitness and just sitting outside in the parking lot, contemplating what to do. I was too ashamed to close it down. My pride kept me paying my two employees and the monthly bills.

Finally, after weeks of agonizing over what people would say about me, I made the very tough and excruciating decision to close the gym and say goodbye to my dream. The day I closed the gym was one of the saddest days of my life. I had worked so hard and failed so miserably. I had no space for all of the new gym equipment I had recently purchased, so I had to have a fire sale to get rid of it. On the Saturday of the closing, I watched strangers, friends, enemies, and a few nut jobs pick over my stuff and load it up into their trucks, back seats and mini vans. I felt like such a failure, but it had to be done. My run as the Fitness King had come to a screeching halt.

After the gym closed, I turned my attention to being the best educator I possibly could. At our school, like most urban schools in America, we had a terrible time convincing fathers to participate in any of the school functions. This was especially true of parent-teacher conferences, where we needed them the most. We must have tried everything, from coupons to local restaurants, gift cards, and school t-shirts, to special drama performances by the kids, but nothing seemed to drive the numbers. So I set out with the crazy idea to drive the most father participation in the history of the school. I designed an event called the Men's All-Nighter. The rules were simple: $10 to attend, no women allowed, and all students had to be accompanied by a male adult. I invited uncles, estranged fathers, big brothers, granddads—anyone who fit the bill. Initially, I received some resistance from the powers that be. They were skeptical about having the school open all night, because they thought it might be targeted for theft, as well as concerned there might be injuries and liability issues. But when the permission slips came pouring in, they changed their minds quickly.

On the day of the Men's All-Nighter, over 400 men showed up to the school. We partied, played, and had workshops like Proper Hygiene for Young Men, Self Defense Training and even Hustle Lessons. One of the dads who worked for Home Depot sponsored a carpentry workshop that was outstanding. He actually brought wood and other raw materials to the school and showed the boys and the fathers how to build a mini-garage.

The boys loved it! We also watched movies all night and had

a Midnight Basketball Tournament, Sons vs. Fathers and NOBODY slept. We told the kids at the start we were staying up all night long, and they held me to my word. It was an incredible night, not just for the kids, but for the men as well. For some, because of custody battles or relationship issues with the mothers, this night was the only time they had spent with their sons. In some cases the father had been incarcerated and never had the time to bond with his son, until the Men's All-Nighter. We discovered a lot of the men were intimidated by the school and felt like their opinions didn't matter. Well, after the All-Nighter was over, I encouraged the fathers to start a Men's Club at the school, which ended up being a success. The Men's All-Nighter ended that morning at 10:00 a.m. with a milk, cereal, sausage, egg, toast, and bagel breakfast buffet prepared by the fathers.

A few weeks after the dust settled on the Men's All-Nighter, my good friend Darryl Rogers asked me if I had heard Detroit Public Schools was looking for candidates to fill leadership positions throughout the District. He told me that after pulling off the Men's All-Nighter, I would make a great assistant principal. I laughed it off, until I saw the starting salary, which was $62,000. I jumped all over it. I was so excited to be in the hunt. Even though I had only been teaching for three years, I thought my leadership skills would make up for my lack of experience and my not quite satisfying a few of the requirements (five years of teaching experience being one of them).

My first interview was something out of the Twilight Zone. It was at a middle school with security guards and metal detectors.

I was so eager, I arrived at the school about an hour and thirty minutes before my interview was scheduled to begin. I'm glad I did, because I knew before they called me in this school wasn't a place I wanted to be. The kids were cursing, yelling, fighting, throwing up gang signs, and even smoking in the open. I have to admit I was a little afraid, because I had never seen a school so out of control before. What I saw next took the cake. Right in front of me the principal had a shouting match with three young ladies and a parent—one of the girls had broken the windshield on the principal's new Cadillac. She came running down the hall with a golf club threating the three girls, while the mother stood in the middle of the hall with Mace and a switchblade.

After the melee was over, the principal greeted me like what I had just witnessed was the most normal thing in the world. She called me into her office, and I thought, *oh my God, I hope she doesn't have the freaking golf club in there.* I couldn't believe what came out of her mouth next.

"Good afternoon, Mr. Edison. We're so glad you're here to interview for the physical education vacancy. We've been looking for a good gym teacher for a long time now." I was flabbergasted. *Gym teacher? I'm not here to be the darn gym teacher. Every black man with a teaching certificate that exercises to stay in shape does not want to teach gym, good grief!* I told her there must be some sort of mix up, because I was here to interview for the assistant principal position. Can you believe she laughed out loud right in my face?

"I'm sorry, Mr. Edison, but you can't be older than 25. There is no way you could be the assistant principal at this school, or any other school, for that matter. You haven't been teaching long enough. You're still wet behind the ears! Maybe 10 years from now, when you become a little more seasoned, apply again and then you should have some luck. Thanks for coming in."

I thanked her for her time, but I told her she would see me soon at the next administrators' meeting—if she still had a job. I actually walked out of the meeting pumped up. I couldn't wait to get to the next interview.

Over the next fourteen months I interviewed at 13 different schools. All of them gave me some sort of excuse as to why they didn't want to hire me, but I was unfazed. By the eighth interview, I had mastered the interview questions. I knew exactly what the interview committee was going to ask me before they opened up their mouths. I kept my head up. I knew sooner or later I was going to find a committee that loved me. Over 50 positions were open in the district and I was only on number 14, so I was still fired up.

My fifteenth interview was with Katherine B. White Elementary School. I did my background research on the school and found out it was the largest K-5 school in the state: 1,150 children, two lunchrooms, and three assistant principals. This place was as big as a high school, and it was perfect, extremely clean and well run. The principal was a long-time educator named Linda Edwards whom I had met previously at a district function.

When I arrived to interview, I immediately noticed five other candidates waiting in the hall. I thought to myself, *man, this is going to be a long shot, but I'm up for the task.* I just need the committee to fall in love with me and see my potential, not just my resume.

After about 90 minutes, the committee chair came out.

"Mr. Edison, you're next. Welcome to Katherine B. White Elementary School."

I walked into the interview room and my heart dropped. There were 30 people sitting in a horseshoe with a lone chair at its focal point. I didn't realize the staff of Katherine B. White was over 125 people, and these 30 represented a sample of the entire White Elementary family. Grades K-5, school safety, lunch program, parents, local community organizers, and volunteers.

I took a deep breath, sat down, and went to work. By the time I was done with the panel, they were eating out of the palm of my hand. They loved me and I loved them. I walked out feeling confident like I had just scored a touchdown. Then the committee chair told me, "Mr. Edison, you did great, but we have 15 candidates to interview. We will get back to you and let you know as soon as we can." In my head I was screaming, 15 candidates?? But the next morning when I was getting ready for work my phone rang and it was Linda Edwards with some of the sweetest words I have ever heard a person speak.

"Even though you lack the experience of some of the other candidates, we really appreciated your enthusiasm, energy, and attitude. I would like to officially offer you the position of assistant principal of White Elementary School. Mr. Edison, you're hired."

"Mr. Edison . . . Mr. Edison, hello, hello…?" Finally I came to my senses.

"You had me at you're hired!"

She burst into laughter. In October of 2000, I started my new position as assistant principal of Katherine B. White Elementary School.

CHAPTER 10

New
BEGINNINGS

"Good Seasons start with Good Beginnings."

-SPARKY ANDERSON

To my surprise, at age 27, I had become the youngest assistant principal in the history of the Detroit public school system. This was an exciting time for me—a new position in leadership, a new school and, best of all, a new lady in my life (my relationship with Carla sadly hadn't survived my hectic Chili's/bus attendant/ full-time student schedule). I met Angie coming out of church. It was a lovely summer day, and there she was, beautiful, 5 feet 9, super model gorgeous with long black hair. I stopped her and asked her if she wanted to go to lunch and she agreed, but she insisted on separate cars. I didn't care because this girl was fine! After that lunch Angie and I were inseparable. We spent practically every day together. We would talk for hours about her faith and how she loved going to church. She really helped me strengthen my faith in God, and I loved that about her. I also loved that she was athletic. She ran five miles a day and was in great shape. We even worked out together; she was the first girlfriend I had who liked working out as much as I did. We liked the same type of movies, the same type of food—she couldn't be more perfect. It felt good to be in love and to have someone that loved me.

I was so excited to start work in the fall that I couldn't sleep at night! I practiced getting up on time for weeks before school started. Angie thought I was crazy for doing that, but I didn't care. My first day on the job set the tone for what was to come. I arrived two hours and thirty minutes early—I was determined to be the first one at work and the last one to leave. Bright and early at 8:15 a.m. I was in the hall directing traffic, greeting parents and making sure that the halls were safe. Then out of the corner of my eye I noticed an older, tall, heavyset African woman wearing what looked like a muumuu coming down the hall with me locked in her sights. She walked directly up to me with a scowl on her face.

"Hey you! Are you the new assistant principal?"

"Why yes I am, how may I help you?" I replied cheerfully.

"Come on in your office and sit down, I have something to tell you!"

I was in shock. She's inviting me into *my* office? It should have been the other way around, right? I thought to myself! But, I entertained her request and went in and sat down. She stood over me, hand on hip and said:

"My name is Ms. Jenkins and I have been working at this school for thirty- FO years. I'm on the Fif- FLO in room three- three- FO. So don't you even think about coming up there getting me to change anything! I'm going to do what I want, when I want and how I want, and ain't nobody going to tell me different, you got it, young whipper-snapper?" With that she turned to walk away, but then she had second thoughts and turned back.

"Besides, you can't tell me anything. I have a pair of underwear older than you! So keep all of your bright ideas to yourself, and we will get along just fine. You got it??"

Then she began to sashay out of my office and into the hallway.

I was temporarily paralyzed. Ms. Jenkins had caught me totally off guard. After a stunned moment I jumped up and followed her down the hallway.

"Ms. Jenkins, ma'am, I have only one suggestion."

"Yes?"

"I suggest that if you have a pair of underwear that's over 27 years old, you need to go and get you some new ones. Change is coming and I'm bringing it!"

After that initial encounter, Ms. Jenkins and I became very good friends. Other than that minor incident with Ms. Jenkins, my first year at White Elementary School was magical! My schedule was 7 a.m.–7 p.m. and I loved every minute of it. I was in charge of the lunch program, noon hour aides, early morning absence reports, and I worked with teachers to make sure that they had all the necessary supplies, like books, paper, chalk, and glue sticks. I was able to implement several programs for fathers at the school. Could it be that I had the perfect job? It wasn't even 10 minutes from my house!

That year Wayne County Community College asked me to be the year 2000 Wayne County Spokesman for success, an award also shared by television star and celebrity Greg Mathis, of the TV show Judge Mathis the year previously.

The college sent a television crew out to the school to feature me on the commercial featuring past graduates. It was my first time on local television, and the whole process just thrilled me. Three guys and one young lady showed up to the school with lights, cameras, a boom mic, and a makeup bag. I brought three of my best suits to school because I wasn't sure what look to go for. I asked the producer what color showed up best on camera. "Blue always looks good," he said, so I sprinted to the Teachers Lounge bathroom and changed into my three-button dark blue suit. Next the makeup artist started doing my face, and she scolded me because I couldn't stop grinning. I was so excited to be a part of this commercial.

Next we walked down the halls and into classrooms getting live footage. After a few hours of touring the school we ended up back in my office for the final shoot. The producer told me, "Jonathan, just talk naturally and let the viewers know why you love what you do." I talked for about four minutes, which seemed more like four seconds and then he yelled cut. Once we wrapped, a deep feeling of pride and accomplishment came over me.

About 30 days later, as soon as the commercial aired, my phone rang off the hook with congratulatory calls. To my surprise, I also began to receive invitations in the mail at the school from community service programs to share my story. I couldn't believe that people were actually interested in hearing what I had to say, but during my talks, I would look into the faces of the audience and see that they were genuinely inspired. It was exhilarating, and I had never experienced anything like it.

After my third speaking invitation, I was hooked on the feeling of inspiring people. Seeing the transformations in the eyes of the audience participants gave me such a rush. I also really enjoyed the testimonials of the audience members who told me after hearing my talk they were genuinely motivated and inspired to do something different.

After one speech a guy came up to me and said, "Jonathan, you're really good at this. You should consider becoming a professional motivational speaker." I thanked him for his kind words and shrugged it off. But as the weeks went by, the idea of becoming a professional speaker began to consume me. Even though I had a great job, I started complaining about it instead of being thankful for what I had. Then my best friend Darryl Rogers suggested that I attend a lecture to see a real pro in action: Les Brown. At the time, he was ranked as one of the top motivational speakers in the world, and he even had his own talk show, The Les Brown Show. He was amazing. Watching him present, I could imagine myself on stage just like him. After his lecture, we met and talked about the possibility of my becoming a professional speaker. That night, I made a declaration to the universe that I wanted to become a motivational speaker.

But I was between a rock and hard place because I was still committed to being a great educator, so I put the idea on the back burner. I was still enrolled at Wayne State, and I had just received a brochure in the mail from Harvard University highlighting a new program in their education department for young teachers interested in becoming superintendents in urban schools. I looked at that brochure and thought wow, what a great opportunity that would be. So I forged ahead. But during my second year, things began to go sideways.

My principal, Linda Edwards, called me into her office one day after the Christmas break and asked me several questions regarding my performance and my dedication to the job. I explained I was dedicated, but I was also interested in continuing my education so that I could prepare myself to be a superintendent in the near future.

She lost it. She read me the riot act.

"Jonathan, it seems that you're not focused on the task at hand. The most important thing for you to do right now is to focus on your job and not on the future. You're trying to move too fast and you're going to find yourself on the outside looking in if you don't cut out the distractions and focus 100 percent on your job. I didn't hire you to be in class three days a week. I need you here! So you have to make a decision on what you want to do and what's important to you."

I left the meeting heartbroken. This was the same woman that gave me a shot and told me that the sky was the limit! When Linda hired me, she was excited I wanted to continue my education. We even discussed my attending classes in the evening during my interview. How could she now be upset at me for wanting to further my education? But in her mind she wanted me to be available 24 hours a day, just like her. After that meeting, our relationship went downhill. She single-handedly drained the excitement and exhilaration right out of me. I was never the same afterwards. I couldn't stand the sight of her. I even hated driving up to the building. What was I to do?

At the end of the year I decided that enough was enough, and I asked her politely to sign my transfer papers. But instead of granting my transfer, she forced me to return for another year out of spite. I was devastated. I couldn't believe that she wouldn't just sign the transfer and allow me to move on with my life. Luckily, our school was so large, it was easy to avoid her most of the time as long as I stayed busy. I made sure that I did my job, but working with her was a nightmare.

Finally, the end of the school year came and I received some news that gave me hope — Linda Edwards was retiring!!!! But even as I celebrated, my exuberance was quickly extinguished because the woman Linda had trained for over ten years, Mrs. Louis, was taking over. It was just like working for Mrs. Edwards all over again. Mrs. Louis and Mrs. Edwards shared the same attitude towards my extracurricular pursuits. So even though she was retiring, she somehow still managed to be a rock in my shoe.

I was bored out of my mind and miserable. I started complaining about my job to everyone I knew. I wanted out, but I couldn't figure out how to do it on my own. Little did I know that the universe was going to help me out with my request.

That year the school board voted in a new school superintendent, Dr. Kenneth Stephen L. Burnley. He vowed to make Detroit Public Schools a better place for children, families, and employees. This was a tall order for any new superintendent. Our school district had great teachers and smart kids, but the leadership was terrible.

Just before the end of the first semester, the office of Human Resources sent a fax to all the schools announcing a mandatory meeting that afternoon for all administrators at the Kettering High School gymnasium.

When I arrived the gym was packed with over 500 administrators from all across the District. This group included principals, assistant principals, department heads, and staff coordinators. As I walked through the gym to find a seat the whispers and murmuring was at an all-time high. I found a seat in the bleachers, and soon the head of Human Resources appeared on the stage.

"Ladies and gentlemen, please allow me to have your attention. If I call your name, you are being terminated and reassigned. But rest assured, everyone here is a certified teacher, and we have found you a position within the district that lines up with your certification. Please listen for your name, and if your name is called, make your way over to the blue table to sign for your termination and to receive your new teaching assignment. If you refuse to sign and take a new teaching assignment, we will be forced to terminate you permanently from Detroit Public Schools."

That thirty-second speech sent a shock wave through everyone in attendance. Once she stopped talking a gasp of disbelief echoed through the gym. *No way would they move me, though,* I thought. I was the year 2000 Wayne County Community College Spokesman for success. I was the youngest assistant principal in the history of Detroit Public Schools. No way was I on the chopping block! In the next five minutes three names were called. Mrs. Garrett, Mr. Van, and the third name called was **Mr. Jonathan Edison of White Elementary School.** I couldn't believe it. My head was spinning and my stomach was doing cartwheels. It seemed as if time itself had stood still, but I also felt a weird sense of relief. I stood up and made my way to the exit.

"Mr. Edison, where are you going?" one of the district executives called out.

"I'm going to pursue my destiny," I replied. With a perplexed look on her face, she repeated, "Mr. Edison!!!" I turned around.

"What else are you going to do, hit me in the mouth? Kick me maybe? Ma'am, I'm done!" I yelled.

I made it to the top of the stairs and I pushed the door open to make my way outside and when I looked up in the sky it somehow looked different. I also felt like a 100 lb weight had been removed from around my neck. My shoulders were loose and my face was relaxed for the first time in a looooooong time. When I began to make my way toward the parking lot to retrieve my car my cell phone rang. It was my dad. "Hey, son, are you at work?" he asked.

"Dad, I don't work for Detroit Public Schools anymore."

"What is it that you do now?"

"Dad, brace yourself, I'm going to be a motivational speaker."

"What the hell is a motivational speaker?" he yelled.

I told him that I had been fired and I was not going back to teaching primary school gym, which was the new teaching assignment I had been offered. His advice was simple and straight to the point. "First of all, you better motivate yourself back in there and tell that woman you need a job," he said. "Second of all, I'm not going to give you any assistance. Allow me to remind you that you have a car note, car insurance, light bill, rent, and a bad habit of eating out too much. Do you realize that you have close to $2,000.00 worth of bills before you even have a sandwich?" he asked.

"Dad, I know, but you told me a long time ago that I should always follow my dreams and my heart." We hung up, and I vowed on that day that I would never again put my success in the hands of another human being. I was going to make it happen myself.

One of the first quotes I learned that inspired me then and

continues to inspire me now is by Henry David Thoreau.

"If you advance confidently in the direction of your dreams, and endeavor to live the life in which you have imagined, you will meet with a success unexpected in common hours. You will put some things behind. You will pass an invisible boundary; new, universal and more liberal laws will begin to establish themselves around and within you; or the old laws be expanded, and interpreted in your favor in a more liberal sense, and you will live with the license of a higher order of beings."

The next morning it was official. I was on my own as an entrepreneur—no clients, no background, no prospects, no cards, no website, no nothing! Just a dream, close to $2,000.00 of bills, a disenchanted father, and an upset girlfriend. When I called Angie she went into panic mode.

"What do you mean, you quit your job? What are you going to do? I need a man that has a job, not one with a pipe dream!" she yelled. I tried to calm her down and explain that Detroit Public Schools and Human Resources left me no choice. I was direct and honest. "I have to do this for myself!" I told her. "I can't continue to work for other people, I have to be my own man and work on my own time!" She pleaded with me to go back to work, but I couldn't. I had to strike out on my own.

To become a motivational speaker, the first thing that I had to do was convince myself that I could. So for the next eight weeks I got up every morning at 5:00 a.m. and practiced for six hours straight, reciting quotes and giving pretend lectures on the banks of the Detroit River, which ran behind my house. I went deep into my imagination and visualized the Detroit River as a captive audience hanging on my every word. I imagined the standing ovations, the laughter, the applause, the book signings, the plane rides, the fancy restaurants — I imagined it all. Then reality hit periodically when a ship would pass and blow its horn.

To try and supplement my income I recorded a couple of motivational CDs sharing my best words of encouragement and sold them for $10 a CD. For the next year I made it my mission to speak at as many places as I could for FREE. I knew that the businesses weren't going to come to me, so I had to go to them. It's amazing how many speaking engagements you can secure when you say that it's free. I started with free graduation speeches because I figured that if I had a captive audience of parents, they would purchase my merchandise afterwards or even hire me to speak at their workplaces. Graduation speeches, back yard parties, church revivals, Pizza Hut lobbies, bars, you name it, I did it! I kept my products with me, and I always sold them when I was done speaking. My philosophy at that time was "I will charge them on the way out!"

I was also able to practice my material and hone my platform skills, like timing, stage presence, and my speech closing techniques. A double win for the up and coming motivational speaker.

That year I even wrote my first two motivational books, *Success Is in Your Hands* and *So You're Graduating, Now What?* I was on a mission and I was making great money! I could do a graduation at a high school for free and walk away with two or three thousand dollars in product sales. So I set my sights on doing as many graduation speeches as I could. That year I booked 22 graduation speeches. At this point I had become so good at product sales that I developed a personal development library brand. It was the "I'm Unstoppable Kit." You could get the T-shirt, the bag, both of my motivational CDs, and both of my books for $99.00. At the very beginning and at the very end of my talks I encouraged my audiences to yell "I am Unstoppable! I am Unstoppable! I am Unstoppable!" They went wild every time. And of course 80 percent of the time I sold out of everything.

CHAPTER 11

Who *Wants* to Be a
MILLIONAIRE?

"It comes down to this: If not you, then who?"

-T. HARV EKER

By the summer of 2003, things were going extremely well. I was making great money, Angela and I had gotten engaged, and I had decided I needed a larger apartment. So Angela and I moved into a beautiful one-bedroom apartment with a den. It was on the 8th floor. The moment you walked in, you could see the Detroit River and all of the lights in downtown Detroit. The apartment was in the heart of the city, but tucked away back by the water, so I liked to refer to it as the Bat Cave.

Around the same time, I became aware of the Multimillion Dollar Fast Food King, La Van Hawkins, by reading an article in the *Michigan Chronicle*. He was featured because of his business acumen and his charitable work in the African-American community. The article talked about his successful Burger King and Checkers franchises, and how his businesses had earned over $100 million dollars that year. The article also had a sidebar showing the ten "young entrepreneurs" he had personally assisted in becoming millionaires. La Van gave these ten individuals an opportunity to acquire their own Checkers franchise under his tutelage and to join his management company, La Van Hawkins Food Group. Several weeks after I read that article, his marketing team flooded the radio, television, and billboards with Burger Kings ads featuring the man himself! He appeared in every spot, voiceover, commercial, and billboard ad. He was literally the talk of the town, especially on FM 98 WJLB, where his commercial spots advertising his new Burger King double drive thru spots were in heavy rotation.

One day I was pulling into my parking spot at the Bat Cave and

I saw his fabulous signature black on black Rolls Royce with Burger King plates on it parked nearby. Could it be? *Maybe he's visiting someone,* I thought. I spotted it a few more times over the next week or two, and realized that we actually lived in the same complex. Are you kidding me? The Burger King "King" lives where I live, I thought to myself.

I was coming down on the elevator headed to give a speech at a school in Toledo when I met the Multimillion Dollar Fast Food King himself, for the first time. In the elevator, I was mesmerized by his impeccable dress, his numerous assistants and his beautiful diamond bracelet that lit up the elevator. We made eye contact and I asked him how life was treating him, and in his distinctive baritone voice, he replied, "Absolutely fantastic!". *Ding*—the elevator doors opened and I let him and his entourage go ahead of me. It seemed like they were in a hurry to get somewhere fast. As he made his way to his $500,000 Rolls Royce Corniche convertible, I knew I wanted what he had.

Over the next couple of weeks we ran into each other from time to time, and I would always ask him the same question: "How is life treating you?" His reply was always the same: "Absolutely fantastic!" Shortly thereafter, I picked up the *Detroit News* newspaper and the front page headline was *La Van Hawkins purchases all 91 Pizza Hut locations in Michigan.* He was scheduled to bring in over $300 million in revenue that year. After I saw that article, I told Angie I had to find out his secrets. "This guy lives one floor up from me! All I need is a shot and someone to show me the way, and I can do the rest," I told her.

So for the next week I made it my mission to stalk him—I mean, run into him—again often. Finally, late one Friday evening, I saw his Rolls Royce coming around the corner. I knew he was going to park on the parking deck in the garage, so I cut him off and made sure we would see each other going to the elevator. He was looking very sharp in a blue custom tailored suit and matching blue alligator skin boots.

"Jonathan, hey man, how you doing? How's life treating you?" he asked.

"It will be absolutely fantastic if you show me the way to make a million bucks!" I replied.

He looked at me and laughed. Then he asked me a question that I was dying to hear.

"What can I do for you?" *Jackpot!*

I felt like I had hit the lottery or won a new car, because this was the guy everyone wanted to get close to, and he was directly talking to me!

I replied, "If a young man with a lot of talent, intelligence, and a whatever-it-takes attitude came to you, could you teach him how to be a millionaire like yourself?"

He stepped back, looked me up and down, took a long pause, and then it happened.

"Call my assistant Judy right now 313-595-6001 so we can get started on this Million Dollar dream of yours," he replied. Then we slapped hands, bumped shoulders, and I watched those blue boots stride jauntily away. On the inside I was screaming like I had won a NBA Championship, but I kept cool until he got on the elevator.

Did that really just happen? I couldn't believe it — a shot at the big time! I ran up eight flights of stairs and told Angie and she couldn't believe it either. "We are about to be RICH! Girl do you hear me we are about to be RICH!!" I yelled with excitement.

In one elongated breath, I told her the entire story and then I ran to my bedroom to call Judy, La Van's assistant, to set up the appointment. Surprisingly, she told me that Mr. Hawkins wanted to see me first thing in the morning. Wow, this guy is fast I thought.

The next day at 6:00 a.m. I got up bright and early to meet him for a 9:00 a.m. meeting at his headquarters on Shelby & Congress in downtown Detroit. When his assistant walked me in, I couldn't believe my eyes. This black man was the CEO of a $300 million company run from downtown Detroit. Everything in the office looked like it was out of the *Rob Report* magazine. All the furniture was custom made. The halls were lined with photos of Mr. Hawkins and some of the most influential people in the world: former President Bill Clinton, Nelson Mandela, and Aretha Franklin. He even had a wall titled the Millionaire Hall of Fame. These were pictures of all the young African-

American entrepreneurs he had made into millionaires.

When I met Mr. Hawkins in his office, he wore a custom tailored Pizza Hut shirt, an unbelievable diamond watch, and a pair of Ostrich cowboy boots that cost more than my car.

"Jonathan, let's get down to business. What's on your mind?" he asked. I said I was a young entrepreneur, and I wanted nothing more than to become a millionaire. I told him about my educational background, my credentials, and my current speaking business.

We talked about my schedule. I told him I was doing speeches here and there, but I was really interested in becoming super rich. Then he asked me the million dollar question.

"Are you sure this is what you want?"

I paused for a moment, flashed a mega-watt smile.

"Yes, sir, it is."

"Alright, then, let's make it happen. I want to offer you a position with my company as an R&D specialist and as my personal assistant."

R&D specialist? I didn't know what an R&D specialist was, but I figured I could learn. I was willing to learn whatever I had to learn and do whatever I had to do to get rich.

"Yes, we are about to do the largest LBO *(Leveraged Buy Out)* since Reginald Lewis."

L.B.O? Reginald Lewis? *(First African-American Billionaire and Former CEO of Beatrice Foods)*

"Yes, boy, keep up, you're in the big leagues now! I want you to be in charge of pulling together all the data and packaging it so we can present it. But, your first order of business is to go get me some lunch, take the Rolls to have it detailed, and read this report so we can begin strategizing."

The report was one hundred pages long. Not only was I in, I was in deep! My friends and family couldn't believe it! How did I go from being fired to rolling with the #1 guy in Detroit, driving around in a Rolls Royce and learning from him?

Our time together was always an adventure. He lived such a big lifestyle; every day seemed like something out of a movie or a Jay Z rap video. My first important assignment was to pick up Dionne Warwick and Burt Bacharach from the airport, because they were performing at a private function he was hosting for a group of potential investors. Then the next week we were entertaining the finance committee for Kwame Kilpatrick, a young, dynamic politician who was running for mayor of Detroit.

The ultimate happened one morning when he called me at 4:00 a.m.

"J, I need you to meet me downstairs at 6:00 a.m. Get the Bentley ready, and wear a dark suit, because we have a meeting in Chicago at 10:00 a.m. and we have to be back in Detroit by 1:00 p.m."

I was on it! The next thing I knew we were on a private jet outbound for Chicago. At the front of the plane was a captain's chair with La Van's initials and personal logo embossed in the center of it. The breakfast plates were trimmed in gold with his name engraved in the center. As I ate my eggs and bacon, I couldn't believe this dude's name was on the freaking plate in gold—*Are you kidding me?!*. While La Van talked business on the phone, I just stared out the window, allowing my imagination to run wild. I kept telling myself one day I was going to have my own plane with my own monogrammed breakfast plates. My thoughts were interrupted by La Van's baritone voice.

"J, we're here. Let's get ready to go make these millions!!!"

He told me to go ahead of him and right before I walked down the steps he yelled, "J. . . How do I look?"

"Like a million bucks, sir!" I said very confidently.

"Sho you right!" he replied. We hopped into the limo and went to the meeting. I had never seen thirty white guys in blue suits in one room at the same time before. It looked like a bankers' convention, and these guys were sharp! They talked numbers, projections, scenarios, and how they were going to structure the deal. La Van was excited. You could see the determination in his face. If he pulled off this deal, it would make him a billionaire overnight. The plan was to do a leveraged buyout of AFC Enterprises, which included Popeye's Chicken, Churches' Chicken, Seattle Coffee, and Cinnabon. Collectively, they made up an organization of over 5,000 stores and over 2 billion dollars in sales. The plan was to get the deal structured, raise the capital, close the deal, and break the company into pieces. By selling the company in small clusters of stores, the profit would be maximized, bringing in more revenue than selling the entire company or each store individually.

Back in Detroit, we had to meet with city officials and make it to the city inspection of La Van's newest venture, Sweet Georgia Brown. Sweet Georgia Brown was an upscale 5-star bistro featuring live entertainment, an in-ground aquarium, and the finest wines from around the world. After the inspection we went back over to the office to take a few minutes to plan for the next day. I went out to pick us up a late dinner, and when I returned, La Van was on the phone talking to Bob Johnson, the billionaire CEO of BET, about the return he could earn if he contributed capital to the deal. The numbers were stratospheric. *Wow,* I thought. *I wonder what would happen if I invested?* La Van hung up the phone.

"J, we're getting close!"

I thought to myself, *this is my shot. I'm going to take it!*

I asked him about the return rate for investors and how much money he needed to broker the deal. He explained he needed to raise $200 million cash. A potential investor with as little as $50,000 could become a millionaire once the deal closed. Then I asked the magical question.

"La Van," I said, "So if I had $50,000 dollars to invest, you're telling me in two years or less I could be a millionaire and have equity in a billion dollar company?"

"Absolutely!"

That night I went home and told Angie about the deal. I called my father and explained to him what I was about to do. Angie pleaded with me not to risk so much money, but I knew it was what I wanted. My father asked if I was absolutely sure I wanted to go through with it, and if I trusted La Van to do the right thing.

"Absolutely, pops! We're about to be rich!" I said.

So the next day I took every penny I had, including a $30,000 loan from my father, and I invested $50,000 into the Hawkins Food Group. On the morning I made the investment La Van looked at me and smiled. My father and La Van shook hands and then La Van and I almost simultaneously signed the binding investment contract.

"Welcome to the club," he said.

"The club?" I asked with a look of bewilderment on my face.

"Yes, the **Millionaires' Club.** Your life is never going to be the same, young man."

I spent the next two months in Chicago doing R&D work and learning about the operation side of the business. Once the deal went through, I was going to be the proud poppa of 25 of my own franchise stores. As the weeks flew by my life was a whirlwind: planes, trains, automobiles, hotels, dinners, plays, functions, events, fundraisers, championship fights. You name it, I had access to it. On Angie's birthday, which happened to be two days before mine, La Van called me.

"J, take the Rolls for the weekend and stop by the box office downtown. I have tickets waiting for you for the Cars and Stars event."

I was living in a dream world. I had it all, and without question, I was on my way to making millions of dollars and buying my own plane and having my own monogrammed plates. By the summer of 2003, we were rolling. Sweet Georgia Brown was packed every night with Detroit's elite, the financing for the LBO was almost finalized, and we were making plans to relocate our headquarters to Atlanta.

But in August, everything started to come unraveled. Creditors, employees, vendors, and even the landlord of the Hawkins Food Group office started complaining about not being paid.

Then during mid August the local media ran a story about La Van owing Norman Yatooma, a prominent Detroit attorney, hundreds of thousands of dollars in unpaid legal fees over a Burger King settlement. When the story broke, my phone started blowing up.

That same night Norman Yatoomah and the local news were outside of Harbortown Apartments with police, bailiffs from the 36th District Court and moving vans. Attorney Yatoomah was there to collect. Armed with a court order to break down La Van's door if he didn't pay up. It was a circus. Flanked by the Detroit police and a locksmith, Yatooma broke down La Van's door and loaded all his valuables onto a moving truck. *How could this be happening?* I thought. I stood outside with the rest of the onlookers and watched them remove La Van's king-size-bed, jewelry, all of his shoes, artwork, a custom jukebox, living room furniture, several fire arms, and even the groceries out of his refrigerator. This attorney Yatoomah was not playing around!

I asked a police officer on the scene where they were taking all of his things, and he explained to me that they were taking La Van's belongings to the city airport to be auctioned off later that evening.

I frantically called La Van, but I didn't get an answer. I flew down to the headquarters but when I tried to ring the buzzer the power was off. I didn't know what to do or where to look! At last, several hours later, I went by Sweet Georgia Brown's. I found La Van there and told him what was going on. Calmly, he told me not to worry. It was all under control.

"It's just an oversight," he said.

"Oversight! This dude took your suits, your shoes, your bed, your furniture, and all your valuables and sold them at an auction! Are you freaking kidding me? What are we going to do?" I yelled.

He told me to calm down. I was being dramatic, and this was just a wave we needed to ride out before the big deal went through.

"Ok," I said, "But this entire situation is making me very uncomfortable."

Then a thought flashed in the back of my mind and I could hear Angie's voice.

"I told you investing with him was a bad idea; you should have listened to me!"

Listen to you! Aren't you the same one that was riding around in his Rolls Royce with me? We argued for days about this. Eventually, I asked her to move out, because I was sick of hearing how silly I was for making that decision.

After she moved, things were a little quieter. I concentrated on helping La Van finalize the deal. Little did I know this pulled thread was the beginning of the unraveling of our relationship. In November and December we continued to work. We ignored the press and all the negative attention coming in. I definitely felt uneasy after the Burger King story and the Yatoomah auction. In the pit of my stomach, I knew it was over, but we were laser beam focused on getting the deal done. I stayed along for the ride until I overheard him on a conversation telling someone he thought the FBI was watching him and he could be indicted at any moment! When I heard that, it scared me half to death. The FBI? Indictments? I knew I needed to get out of there and away from him immediately. A few days later, I told him I wanted out. I wasn't prepared to go to jail and have the FBI watching my every move.

"La Van, I need my money back, and I need it now," I said.

Always the good poker player, he didn't flinch. He asked me if I was sure I wanted to give up, knowing we were so close.

"Absolutely," I replied. "I have to get out and I need my life's savings back." On January 3, 2004 he reached into his pocket, pulled out his checkbook, and wrote me two checks for $25,000 each. He dated one check 1/16/2004 and the other check 2/25/2004. I didn't give the dates too much thought. I figured he might need time to move some money around. Little did I know he was buying himself time to BS me. On January 16, I tried to deposit the first check into my account. The bank manager came out and said we needed to talk.

"Mr. Edison, the account you're attempting to draw from has been closed. We cannot allow any activity at this time."
I passed out right there in the bank. The teller had to call an ambulance. When I came to, the paramedic told me I fell out of the chair and hit my head on the desk and that I might have a mild concussion.

I left the bank, sat in my car ,and cried for what seemed like an hour. How could this be happening? What did I do to deserve this? What was I going to do now? What were my friends going to think? Question after question ran through my mind.

I thought things couldn't get any worse, but I was wrong. That night Angie came over to stay for the weekend, or so I thought. She actually came by to get the rest of her things.

"John, this is way too much for me, and you need to get your life together. You've lost all your money, and all of your friends are saying bad things about you. You're not the same. I'm leaving you. I hope you have a good life, and I hope you find what you're looking for. Goodbye."

Within 48 hours my entire life came crashing down and my emotions began to implode .

CHAPTER 12

Deep *Deep*
DEPRESSION

"Life is not about waiting for the storm to pass,
it's about learning how to dance in the rain."

-ANON

I fell into a deep, deep depression. I felt like I was paralyzed from the neck down. My head and stomach hurt constantly, my vision was blurred, and my body ached all over. I spent every day on my couch with the curtains drawn watching soap operas and People's Court. I must have gained over 40 pounds. I ate myself into a coma every day—ice cream, pizza, gas station sandwiches —anything $5 could buy became my daily diet. At night I began binge drinking. Red wine, champagne, tequila, it didn't matter —anything that could numb the pain of my defeat. Weekends ran into weeks and weeks never seemed to end. If I wasn't on the couch watching television, I was sitting at the window looking out over the Detroit River with a glass of wine or champagne in my hand, doing my best to drown my sorrows.

Although I suffered from every symptom of depression, I was in total denial. A few of my close friends tried to get me to leave the house and participate in a few activities, but I always said no. I wasn't prepared to answer any questions about what happened with La Van and with Angie. By this time I had heard through the grapevine La Van skipped town and Angie was dating a bunch of different guys. NBA superstar Jalen Rose was the latest man in her life. When I heard that, I really spiraled out of control, and went into what I like to call my alter ego. That's E-Diddy mode. You know, P. Diddy.

Of course we're all familiar with the popular and talented Diddy, aka Puff Daddy, aka Sean Combs. Well, deep within the reservoir of my super ego, I created a personification of him in the form of E. Diddy. E. Diddy loved women, champagne, hot tubs, and late nights. E. Diddy had my body, but my mind and heart were somewhere else, somewhere Jonathan couldn't reach. After weeks of nonstop partying, I was finally brought back to reality when a letter appeared underneath my door informing me I owed over seven thousand dollars in back rent and late fees, and that if I didn't pay in two weeks, I'd be evicted.

Holy crap! I was going to lose my beautiful riverfront apartment? I got myself together, because there was no way I could relinquish the Bat Cave. I worked so hard to get here and now it was slipping through my fingers. I checked the stash I kept in the closet and realized I only had $948.00 left to my name. E. Diddy had exhausted my last $10,000 partying, drinking, and feeling sorry for myself. The next morning I got up at 5:00 a.m. and I prayed for help. Then I put my shoes on and went outside for a run to clear my mind. I must have run for hours around the Harbortown complex, racking my brain on how to come up with close to $8,000 in two weeks. I called a few schools and tried to schedule a few quick speeches and hopefully sell some products, but no one hired me. Then I tried to borrow the money from the bank. They refused. Pretty soon only 24 hours remained before I had to pay up or get out! This was it. The end of my run. I didn't have any more moves to make.

Then my dad called and asked me how I was doing. I just broke down in tears.

"Dad, I'm a failure. I've lost all of my money, Angie is gone, and Harbortown is going to evict me in the morning."

My dad didn't even flinch. "How much do you owe?" he asked.

"$7,450.00"

"Son, don't worry about it. You're not a failure. You're just having a run of bad luck, and anyone who has done anything significant in life experiences what you're experiencing. Can you drive over now and pick up the money?"

Shoot, I started running over there until I remembered I had a car! When I arrived at my dad's house a few minutes later he handed me $10,000 in cash.

"Sign this." He handed me a promissory note that he had drafted with a schedule for repayment.

"This is your promissory note, because that's what this is, a loan, and I want my money back in a timely manner, so you better get busy!"

I signed the paper, snatched the cash and flew over to the bank and to my rental office. The Harbortown folks had been rooting for me, but they couldn't believe I had come up with the money. When I dropped off that check, it was like an elephant had been lifted off my chest. My prayers had been answered. I was renewed. I had been gifted an opportunity to start over and get it right this time. I no longer felt the need to mourn the loss of a failed business venture and a partner that didn't want to be with me anymore. I was young, ambitious, and hardworking, and I wasn't about to allow a $50,000 loss and a sudden break up to define who I was.

CHAPTER 13

Would the *Real* JE Please
STAND UP?

"Every man is a divinity in disguise."

-RALPH WALDO EMERSON

When I walked out of that rental office, I felt like a ton of bricks had been lifted off my back. Thanks to my dad, I no longer had the burden of where I was going to live weighing me down. Until this day only a few people knew about my depression and my out of control downward spiral. It's funny. I never knew the stigma that was associated with depression in the black community. Mainly because if you live within the African- American community and you have a problem, your friends, parents, and elders will tell you to take your problems to the Lord and lay them on the altar. No one ever says maybe you should seek professional help for your condition. If you have a toothache, you go and see a dentist. If you have a water leak, you call a plumber. If you want a five course meal, you call a chef. If you want to build a new home, you call a contractor. But, if you are having *mental issues* in the African-American community, you're instructed to call your pastor. While I'm a *big* believer in the power of prayer and the need for faith, I also know firsthand that depression can be mentally and physically crippling. If you're reading this and you suffer from depression, you have no reason to be ashamed. Don't make the same mistake that I did and lose 6 months of your life because you're embarrassed to share your pain with anyone.

Depression is an imbalance in your life, and a professional therapist or psychiatrist can help you get that balance back. Looking back, I wish I had the courage to go and seek help. You may even discover that you require medication, and that's ok too. Remember that your life doesn't only consist of physical health — it is imperative that you have good mental health as well.

After I paid my rent, I was determined to turn everything around. I had a lot on the line — my pride, my self-worth, my business, and my identity. I needed to shake off my streak of bad luck, pay off my dad as soon as possible, and prove to myself that I was still a winner. Back at my apartment, I sat at my desk and carved out a plan of attack.

The first thing that I did was tally up my leftover funds. I ordered a few hundred books and a few hundred CDs, and then I hit the streets hard. I started speaking any and everywhere that I could. The first week I was able to pull down $800, which gave me a little cushion, but I was still on edge. I had bills to pay and a lot to prove. I had my checkbook open and was anxiously crunching numbers when I received a phone call from a woman that lived on the east side of Detroit.

"Mr. Edison, hi, this is Mrs. Jones, and I saw you at my oldest son's graduation speech last year. You were outstanding. I was wondering if you could speak at my younger son's police cadet graduation in a few days. I know it's last minute, but I really think that you are the man for the job. It's 300 police cadets that could use some motivation!" she said in one long breath.

I was holding my cell phone wondering if I'd have a chance to get a word in. Then she explained she didn't have any money, and there was no budget allocated for a speaker.

"I do have a $93.00 money order that was supposed to go to Detroit Edison, but I'm willing to make it out to Jonathan Edison instead." I laughed.

"Mrs. Jones, you've got yourself a deal. I just need the location, time, head count, and a table to sell my products." She practically leaped through the phone. She couldn't believe that I said YES. What she didn't know is that I would have done it for free just for the chance to sell my products. What a way to close the weekend.

The entire weekend I was like a heavy weight fighter getting ready for a million-dollar prize fight. But instead of shadow boxing and skipping rope, I practiced my delivery and memorized quotes. The morning of the big showdown, I loaded up my trunk with books, CDs, tote bags, and a few leftover T-shirts. I put on my favorite CD—2Pac's "Me Against the World." I pulled away from Harbortown Apartments determined and cool, as if I was walking down the aisle to the boxing ring. At the Northern High School auditorium a front row seat was waiting for me. After a few minutes, I noticed the dignitaries and other important folks taking their places on the stage. As they filed in from behind the curtain, I couldn't believe what I was seeing. It was Dr. Kenneth Stephen Burnley, the new superintendent that had axed me from Detroit Public Schools. I sat there completely flabbergasted. I hadn't seen Dr. Burnley since that day in the auditorium, and I was nervous. But at the same time, I was excited to show my resilience.

"Excuse me, Mr. Edison, we are ready for you to take the stage," said Mrs. Jones. The moment of truth had arrived. I made my way to my seat on stage.

Just then the 300-plus police cadet students filled the auditorium.

They were all very neatly dressed in their police cadet uniforms and full of energy. As they settled into their seats, hundreds of parents, friends, loved ones, and relatives began to fill the auditorium. What a beautiful canvas to paint on, I thought. As I bubbled with anticipation, I felt the need to make a few adjustments to my notes. I reached into my inside pocket and grabbed the 8 ½ sheet of neatly-folded white paper. I wrote at the top, "I AM UNSTOPPABLE." I wrote it again and again and again. I filled the entire sheet of paper up with those three words; each time I wrote the words, I felt a surge of creative energy flow through my body. My forehead began to sweat, my palms moistened. I felt like I could pick up a building. It was the strangest sensation.

While all of this was going on in my world, the program was well underway. Dr. Burnley made the final remarks before I took the podium. He did his same old "kids are our future" speech that most of the audience had heard multiple times. Unimpressive. By this time I was so jacked that I couldn't contain myself in my seat, so I stood up. The director began reading my bio, very slowly, and I quickly became agitated. The next thing that I knew, I yelled out "C'mon, let's get it on!" The entire auditorium erupted in laughter, because they could feel my passion.

I walked slowly up to the podium with a big grin on my face. I felt that surge again shoot through my body. Then something incredibly strange happened. Time stopped. The noise of the crowd disappeared. The space in front of me grew until the people looked like little tiny dots. I could see their faces, but they were so far away. I could feel the heat of the earth beneath my feet, but my entire body seemed to move in slow motion. It was like I orbited out of the room and came back down to watch myself from the rafters, or like I was watching a movie of myself on a widescreen. The best way I can describe what happened on that afternoon was that I had my first out-of-body experience. Then in a flash, I was back at the podium. I looked out into the crowd.

"Someone repeat after me: 'I am unstoppable.'"

The audience was silent. I had no idea what would happen next. Would the crowd respond? Would I be stuck up on the podium with my mouth hanging open like a dummy? That pause was full of tension.

Then over five hundred people yelled back at me.

"I am unstoppable!!"

I instructed the audience to take both hands and point to themselves.

"Now repeat after me, 'I AM UNSTOPPABLE!'"

Again 500-plus voices rang out.

"I AM UNSTOPPABLE!!"

The next 18 minutes were a blur.

"Thank you for having me. I hope that you guys have a fantastic year," I said at the close of my speech. The place erupted. They gave me a standing ovation. I tried to make my way back to my seat, but the entire panel sitting onstage blocked me. Each one of them stood up to shake my hand.

"Great job, young man."

"Wow, that was awesome!"

"Way to go, sir."

I finally reached my seat. I looked to my left and realized that Dr. Burnley's seat was empty. But at that point it didn't matter anymore. I had beaten my lower self into submission.

Just as I began gathering up my things to make it back to my product table someone tapped my right shoulder. I turned around to find another angel from heaven — Cynthia Latoyia Millier, director of the City of Detroit Employment and Training Division. I didn't even know that such a title existed. She handed me her card. It had a note written on the back. "You were amazing. My entire staff needs to hear you. Can we talk?" *Can we talk? Are you serious? We can talk right here right now!*

I asked her what she had in mind, and she wanted to know if

I was available in a few weeks. I told her that I was available in the next few minutes. "I can meet you at your office within the hour, if that works for you," I said.

"Wow, you don't want to waste any time," she replied.

"No, ma'am, that's because I'm unstoppable."

She laughed. "I will see you within the hour, Mr. Edison." I ran back to where my product table was set up outside the auditorium, and it looked like a hundred people were in line. As I was taking off my jacket to sign books, a chant of "I'M UNSTOPPABLE!" broke out. In less than 20 minutes I completely sold out of everything that I had. It was the perfect culmination to a great speech. I looked down at my watch and realized that I had to get moving. I had a date with DESTINY waiting for me. I shook a few more hands and took a few more pictures and then I made a mad dash to the car. I popped the trunk while I was running toward the car, tossed my roller bag in it, and took off. Two quick lefts and six minutes on the freeway stood in between me and this meeting. I arrived at the office and told the young lady sitting at the desk that I was there to meet with the director.

"Have a seat, sir, and I will see if she's available...what's your name?"

I chuckled to myself.
"You can tell her that it's Mr. Unstoppable."

A few moments later, Cynthia emerged from the back and gave me the biggest hug. "I have been telling everyone about you... We can't wait to work with you. C'mon back so we can discuss the details."

When the meeting was over I calmly walked to the elevator. But who could take an elevator at a time like this? I had negotiated a $12,000 contract with a $6,000 deposit. It was the biggest deal I'd ever done. I felt like one of the contestants on The Price is Right when the announcer says, "You've won a new car!!" I bolted for the stairs and ran down the three flights to the lobby as fast as I could. Once I made it to the main floor I shot out of the front door like a rocket. As I ran top speed through the parking lot to my car, I shouted at the top of my lungs, "I'M UNSTOPPABLE!"

That next week I picked up my deposit check. I paid my rent for 3 months and gave my dad the rest. When I handed him the money he said something to me that has stayed with me up until this day.

"John, always stay on top of your game, give your best, and never go out without a fight."

As I reflect back on that day I realized something about myself. The surge of energy that I kept feeling was my higher self, attempting to emerge. The I AM that kept coming was the highest form of expression. I AM is God, and anything that you add to I AM, you become.

I AM **UNSTOPPABLE.**
I AM **WEAK.**
I AM **STRONG.**
I AM **DEPRESSED.**
I AM **EXCITED.**
I AM **A FAILURE.**
I AM **BRILLIANT.**
I AM **CONFUSED.**
I AM **OVERJOYED.**
I AM **OVERWHELMED.**
I AM **POISED.**
I AM **SAD.**
I AM **CONFIDENT.**

As you can see it really matters what you add to it, because that is what comes through.

I was so proud at that graduation, because at last, the real JE had finally stood up.

CHAPTER 14

A *Rude*
AWAKENING

*"Never get comfortable,
because the alarm is going to go off."*

-JONATHAN EDISON

Over the next several years I was having good success in my speaking business. Not only was I selling a ton of products, I was traveling the world and picking up big clients along the way. The first really big client I secured was CVS Pharmacy. The regional vice president, Steven M. Wing, heard me speak at an event in Detroit and found me immediately after my presentation.

"Jonathan, that was incredible," he said. "How would you like to fly to California to speak for a group of my managers?"

I grinned and said "I would love to."

"Give my secretary a call and let's set it up. Are you available on March 16?" he asked. I did everything I could do to pause before answering his question so I wouldn't seem desperate. Beneath my poker face, though, I knew I was available without checking the calendar for the next 5 years.

Several months later at a cocktail party in Detroit, I met an HR executive from Verizon Wireless who happened to be on the planning committee for their upcoming conferences. He was impressed with my work, and he invited me to speak at the Verizon Wireless National Conference, which consisted of 10,000 Verizon Wireless employees from the New York and New Jersey areas. I was scheduled to deliver three ninety-minute workshops, two back-to-back and the final one the following day. When I walked in the room for my first workshop, my jaw dropped to the floor. I was thinking maybe a hundred people or so would show up. There were 1,500 people in the first workshop! *Holy crap,* I thought.

Each workshop had a room attendant, who was in charge of housekeeping, introducing the speaker and delivering the surveys. My room attendant came over and said:

"Ok, Mr. Edison, I will be introducing you in 2 minutes…any last words or requests? This is a tough crowd, and they are usually out for blood."

I stood up, adjusted my tie, straightened my pocket square, and looked deep into her eyes and said. "Let's get it on."

In that next moment it was as if I was shot out of a cannon. I delivered the most energetic, story-filled, and motivating speech of my young career. The audience laughed, cried, and cheered me on. A few even shouted out a couple of hallelujahs and amens.

But at my speech's conclusion I began to notice people getting up and walking out. There were still about two minutes left. Of course that didn't sit well with me, so I yelled "Hey, where are you guys going? I'm almost done!" One enthusiastic lady replied, "I'm going to get in line, before the rush to get your books." Then it hit me, I was about to have the biggest product sale day in my speaking career. I closed the speech, and before I could say thank you and do my famous Dr. King close . . . the room emptied out and the audience headed directly for my product table. Not only did I sell all 500 Unstoppable Kits at $99.99, but I sold an additional 300 books and DVDs. By the time my second presentation was over, I was completely sold out. I couldn't believe it. I sold out of everything in less than 48 hours!

It was a dream come true. Over $23,000 in product sales and a ball room full of people that loved my presentation.

I had spoken for plenty of schools and small businesses, and the CVS job had been a huge step, but this was my first really significant corporate gig speaking to thousands of people. After Verizon, I knew I had made the right decision to become a motivational speaker.

Several weeks after the New York sales blitz, I received a call to speak at a local event near Lansing, MI. It was a cold winter day in November when I made the trip up to Lansing. The roads were covered with snow, so the meeting planner decided I should take a small charter plane up to the event. After the short 20 minute flight we touched down on what looked like a cornfield with a runway attached, and I made my way into the small terminal. Pretty soon I saw a lady holding up a piece of cardboard with my name written on it in black magic marker.

"Hi, that's me, Jonathan Edison," I smiled. The lady looked up at me and turned beet red.

"Are you sure you're Jonathan Edison, the motivational speaker?"

"Yes, ma'am, that's me, in the flesh."

The woman (I'll call her Suzie) didn't say a word. She just turned around angrily, reached for her cell phone and made a call. I was wearing jeans, Timberlands, and a Detroit Lions skullcap, and my first thought was that she was upset because I was dressed so casually. I went to reassure her I was not going to be speaking in street clothes and that I had a suit with me. But that wasn't it. I was about to get the rudest awakening of my life. Right as I leaned over to get her attention, Suzie yelled at whoever was on the other end of the phone, "Oh my God, he's BLACK!!!!!. We can't have a black speaker for this group! Who is responsible for this?" She *yelled* into the phone.

I wasn't sure I had heard her right. I stood there in shock. Then Suzie got off the phone and said, "Mr. Edison, I have something really important to ask you about your visit and presentation. Would you mind not greeting any of the audience participants, taking the back way in, and not coming out on stage until the very last second?" I looked puzzled, I'm sure of it. But in that moment I only had one question.

"Do you have my $2,500.00 check?"

I didn't care who or what the audience was. I knew that I was going to go out and give my best! I figured if they were paying me to do what I loved to do, then I was ready to rock and roll no matter what. Not to mention that I was already there. I had nothing to lose.

"I will give it to you right now if you agree to my terms."

"Let's get it on, then," I said.

A little nervous, I took the back way to the auditorium. The hallways were dusty and the floors very slippery. In the bathroom I whipped out my cell phone and called my dad. I let him know exactly what was going on and where I was, in case I didn't make it out alive. I must have sat behind that stage for two and a half hours before Suzie came to get me.

"Alright, Jonathan, you have about 45 minutes to do your presentation. When I give you the signal, you can come out."

From behind the curtain I could faintly hear her introduce me. The audience began to applaud. I walked out from behind the curtain and said loudly, "Good evening, Michigan Horse Council!"

The room went completely silent. It was so quiet you could hear the buzz from the fluorescent lights in the ceiling. The sixty or seventy white men in the audience were visibly agitated at my presence. I could see their faces turning three different shades of red as I delivered my first 5 minutes. I didn't think I was going to make it out of that place in one piece. The audience was cold and unresponsive. I was doing my best stuff, and not even a chuckle or a half smile crossed one of those faces. But I kept on with my speech. I figured as long as I made it to the forty-five minute mark, I would be ok. I snuck a quick glance at my watch. *Are you serious?* Only 10 minutes had passed. By this time I was sweating everywhere—face, neck, underarms, you name it, if it was on my body it was sweaty. Around the 15 minute mark I felt like I was about to crash and burn at a hundred miles an hour without an eject button.

I'm not sure what it was, but at the 20 minute mark it seemed that I had finally made a small crack in the ice cold room. I began sharing my personal story of perseverance and struggle and I could immediately feel the crowd soften. The more I shared, the more they listened with intent instead of malice. At the 30 minute mark, I looked into their eyes, and I noticed they were watching how hard I was working and they were secretly cheering for me. That's all I needed to bring it home strong. I closed on a high note by reciting one of my favorite quotes by Charles Swindol on attitude. When it was over, the members of the Michigan Horse Council gave me a standing ovation. I was soaking wet and exhausted, but I had made it across the finish line—The 45-minute mark.

Immediately, I turned around to leave the way I came, but Suzie stopped me.

"Jonathan. Wait, they love you. Where are you going?"
I turned around.

"No....they don't love me, because they don't love themselves. Any group of people with that much hate for another human being because of the color of his or her skin can't love anyone or anything.

"That goes for you as well, madam. So thanks but no thanks— I'm out!"

I kept walking and I didn't look back.

At home that night, I sat on my bed and I wept. But I didn't weep for myself, I wept for the struggle. When I was younger I remember my grandmother talking about "THE STRUGGLE" and I never knew what she meant until that day.

What did I just experience within the United States of America in what was now known as the New Millennium? Did racism still exist? Was it dead, was it alive and well?

Honestly, after that experience I really questioned myself and the world that I thought I lived in.

That was my first real encounter with racism, and after that incident with the Michigan Horse Council, I could only imagine what life must have been like for those that had come before me 30, 40, 50, and even 400 years ago.

As horrible as it was, that experience was actually a blessing in disguise. It motivated me and pushed me to study the greatest communicator and freedom fighter this world has ever known, Dr. Martin Luther King Jr.

Over the next several weeks, I listened to his recordings, watched his archived videos, read volumes of his work, and studied his poise from the speaker's platform. During one of my many trips to the Detroit Public Library, I found a quote by Dr. King that sang to me from the pages. It encapsulated my experience, my struggle, and my work ethic.

It promotes excellence, sacrifice and most of all, the strength to override ignorance and racism:

"If a man has been called to be a street sweeper he should sweep streets like Beethoven composed music, He should sweep streets like Shakespeare wrote poetry, He should sweep streets like Michael Angelo painted.

He should sweep streets so well until all the heaven and earth shall stop to pause and say HERE lived a great street sweeper and he did his job well."

If you ever see me speak live, this is the quote I close with for every presentation I deliver. No matter how many times I recite that quote, it always brings tears to my eyes and strength to my soul.

R.I.P. Dr. Martin Luther King, Jr.
Jan 15, 1929 - April 4, 1968

CHAPTER 15

Business, after Business, after
BUSINESS

*"If at first you don't succeed, try, try again. Then quit.
There's no point in being a damn fool about it."*

-W. C. FIELDS

For the next three or four years, business was really steady. I was able to secure a few long-term contracts within several schools and I was on the road at least twice a week. My book sales were still fantastic, but there was a part of me that was unsatisfied with my financial progress. I wanted to have a business empire that provided me with great stability and wealth. My speaking was a great income, but it wasn't going to get me my private jet and gold plates with my name on them. I had the drive, the tenacity, and the energy to pull it off, but I didn't believe that I could meet my goals running only one business. So I set my intention on becoming a diversified entrepreneur.

My very first venture was probably the craziest idea of them all, but I have to admit it sounded pretty good at the time. A longtime friend of mine, Ricky, approached me with an idea that would potentially make both of us rich quick. (Yeah right!)

"J, LISTEN. I gotta great deal that's going to make us rich, my cousin has a connection in China and he said we can order 1 million dish towels from China and sell them here to the Dollar Stores in the United States for a huge profit."

I thought about it, and he was right. If we sold the towels for 50 cents each, it would be a half million dollars for us. I said:

"OK, Ricky, tell me this—how much is it going to cost us?"

"It's only going to cost us $15,000 plus travel expenses to China to have them shipped back."

"OK, so how much is it going to cost *me?*" I said.

"$15,000 plus travel to China!"

"Are you nuts? Where is your half?"

Ricky never had any money, but he always had great ideas on how to spend other people's money. Even so, after a little more convincing I was sold. I called him up and said "Ricky, let's get rich." I gave Ricky the money and waited for 3 weeks. Then Ricky finally called with the great news.

"J, we are the proud owners of 1 MILLION dish towels."

I thought to myself, *I'm about to be rich!* A little over a $17,000 investment and a $400,000+ profit.

I don't know if you've ever seen a million dish towels, but they take up a lot of space. We stored dish towels everywhere. My apartment, his apartment, the trunks of our cars, friends' garages, until we finally broke down and got a storage facility. Now that we had the dish towels, it was time to unload them. Over the next month we must have visited over fifty dollar stores in the Metro Detroit area, but we only made $6,000.00 worth of sales. We couldn't believe it. How could they not be selling like hot cakes? Well, little did we bother to find out, Detroit dollar stores also ordered from the exact same vendor in China, and they got the same dish towels, ten cents for a pack of three.

WHAT??????? ARE YOU KIDDING ME?

I blamed Ricky for not doing the research, but I should have blamed myself for the stupid move. With my business history, I should have known better. I got excited and made a bad decision, strictly on impulse and greed. Over the next two years, we would sell dish towels at festivals, bazaars, and local events, 10 for a dollar. I got so frustrated that most times, I just gave them away so I wouldn't have to drive back to the storage facility. Our last summer of dish towels I rented a U-Haul and picked up a few friends. We drove the streets of Detroit handing out dish towels to anyone that wanted them. I was so sick of paying for that storage unit, I didn't know what else to do. It's funny when I look back on it now, driving around handing out dish towels like a ghetto Robin Hood—WOW. But I guess you live and you learn. (And no, I don't have any dish towels left, sorry.)

My next spontaneous business venture was a little more practical —so I thought. On my honeymoon trip to Hawaii with my wife, I came across a brand of chocolate that knocked my socks off. During our stay at the Trump hotel, a group of local merchants dropped off samples for the guests to enjoy. I looked at the package that was lying in front of my door when we returned from dinner. Hawaiian Host Chocolates. *Wow,* I thought, *that's really nice to give us chocolates like that,* and I promptly forgot about them.

Later that night I ended up having a midnight snack attack. For as long as I can remember, sweets late at night have been my Achilles' heel! This time was no different. When I went into the living room there they were, sitting on the counter. I tore open the package and tried one. This candy was the most glorious chocolate on the planet. I hadn't known it before, but it was clearly true. That chocolate hit my palate and my taste buds went berserk. *WOW this is good,* I said to myself. The next thing I knew, my hand took over my higher functions and kept shoving chocolate into my mouth until they were all gone. I snapped out of it. *Oh my God, did I eat the entire box of 15 specialty chocolates?* YES I DID! After my feeding frenzy I went out on the balcony to think, and that's when it hit me. *I'm going to take these chocolates back to the mainland and turn them into a fund raising venture.* I remembered being the assistant principal of my school and helping out with the fundraising programs. In my part of the world everyone loves Katydids. Katydids were Kathryn Beich Katydids, a delicious blend of caramel and pecans covered in high-quality chocolate. The popular Katydids are based on a recipe created personally by Kathryn Beich, the wife of Paul Beich, who owned the Paul F. Beich Candy Company in Bloomington, Illinois. I noticed that thousands of kids would pedal hundreds of thousands, if not millions, of dollars in chocolate every year in our school district. I knew it; I had seen the fundraising records. Morley Candy was the largest operator in our district. I figured that if I had a superior product, I could give Morley Candy a run for the money.

Once we made it back to the mainland, I got to work immediately, crafting out a plan to start my chocolate empire. I decided that I was going to take the *Netflix vs. Blockbuster* approach and provide the same service as Morley—chocolates—but with a different strategy. Instead of just winning rinky-dink prizes, the kids could win high quality toys. Instead of having to raise $4,000.00 for the grand prize, with us, the seller only had to raise $2,800.00. And to make the deal even sweeter, if you won the grand prize, we would throw in an all-expenses trip for a family of four to Disney world.

Once I had the idea mapped out, it was time to order the candy. I contacted Hawaiian Host Candy Company and placed my initial order of 30,000 units of chocolate. I knew it was a big risk, but the reward was going to be sweet (no pun intended). All I had to do was convince schools to allow us to come in and we would share the profits 65% to 35%, which was actually 5% better for the school than Morley. I created brochures, hired a small staff, and ordered the Mickey and Minnie costumes. That's right, with every school rally that we performed it included a special visit from Mickey and Minnie.

The plan was fool proof; we were outperforming, underbidding ,and overpowering our competitors. My first employee was a young guy that I previously mentored when he was in high school. Terrance Burney, a 6 foot 9 inch smooth-talking fellow that could sell a block of ice to an Eskimo. He was to serve as my #1 sales guy, recruiter, and all around man. He worked the phones, set the appointments, and booked the schools. Both of us were too big to fit into the Mickey and Minnie costumes so we had to hire several small guys and gals to pose as the characters. Within our first two weeks we booked 30 Schools.

They all wanted to see Mickey and Minnie in the flesh. We were riding high, so high that I ordered another 30,000 units to the tune of $20,000 per order. I wasn't fazed, because once we delivered and collected from the 30 schools that we had booked, we were going to clear a minimum of $150,000. Terrance and I couldn't wait to go and collect on the first school. We showed up smiling, ready to count the profit, but the problem was there was no profit. Out of the 900 kids at the school, only eleven returned their order forms. I was in shock. How is it that only eleven kids turned their forms in? I asked the school counselor. She was as stunned as I was, because they were planning to use their profit share to purchase new computers for the computer lab.

Our first collection was a whopping $31.00. But I didn't panic. We had 29 more schools to collect from. Over the next 30 days we collected from school after school, and wouldn't you know it, the same thing was happening all over town. Extremely low return rate. Out of the 30 schools and over 25,000 students, only 212 students returned envelopes. This was a disaster. My American Express card was maxed out and they were looking for me hot and heavy, calling three times a day, asking when I was going to make my initial $20,000.00 payment, which was past due. I didn't panic, but I knew I had to come up with a plan.

Once we delivered the candy orders I earned a total $2,478.00. That was a loooooong way from $150k that I had estimated. Now I was faced with a dilemma: do I try to rock another 30 schools to get rid of the chocolate or do I throw in the towel and start selling the candy door-to-door myself? Guess what I did? If you said rock another 30 schools and go into another $10,000.00 worth of debt, you are correct. The second go around with the 30 schools yielded even less. The first time I chalked it up as a fluke, but this dismal turnout I chalked up as me being in big trouble. But I was determined to find out what the problem was. So at one school that I was really familiar with I set up a meeting with the parent committee to get their feedback. What I found out was astounding. The parent chair of the committee told me that the reason no one participated in the fundraiser is that they thought it was too good to be true. I was so confused. Too good to be true? She cleared her throat and said:

"Mr. Edison, you have to understand that winning a trip to Disney World seemed unrealistic, and most of us thought it was a scam."

I was flabbergasted. "A scam? Are you serious? You guys really didn't believe that you could win the trip?"

"No, not really, so we didn't really give much effort or energy to it."

"Oh!" she added.

Geez, what now, I thought.

"The candy was really good, but we had never heard of it, so we didn't want to order it."

I walked out of that meeting floored by what I had just heard. I thought to myself, *so, if I rip you off, charge you more, give you less service, crummy prizes and bench Mickey and Minnie, I would have sold out?* *Wow.* That was hard for me to digest because if I were a parent I would love to go to Disney World. But my opinion didn't matter. The only opinion that counted was the consumer's.

After that debacle my dad called me over to his house for dinner. When I arrived he said, "John, c'mon in here and let me talk to you, son… can you tell me what it is that you do."

"Dad, I don't understand what you mean. What do I do?" I asked very inquisitively.

"Yes, tell me what it is that you do; I need you to define it and make it clear for me."

Without any hesitation and in the deepest voice that I could muster I stuck out my chest and said, "Dad, I'm an entrepreneur." He laughed, looked down and shook his head and said something that sent shock waves through my body.

"Boy, you're not an entrepreneur, you're an entrepre-NOTHING."

I almost fell out of my chair, but the one thing that I knew is that my dad would never lie to me or sugar coat what he was thinking. My dad was one of the most brutally honest people that I knew. But for him that made life simple. No guessing, bending the truth to make it fit, and definitely no pulled punches.

"What do you mean?" I asked.

He replied, "John, you have all of these businesses and side hustles, and none of them are taking off. You're using one to pay for the other and coming up short in most places. Your focus is off and your attention is divided. Listen, son, it's impossible to be successful if you are a mile wide and an inch deep. You have to focus on what you're passionate about, and not what feels good to say you're doing. Your goal should be to be an inch wide and a mile deep. Because when you do that, mastery becomes a part of the equation. Without mastery you are a 'jack of all trades' and right now you're the #1 JACK. That's why you're not connecting with the 'IT' that you're looking for."

It was like he turned a high-powered hose on my roaring fire. In my mind, I was making moves and making things happen. But in his mind, I was wasting time, money, and effort. That comment sent me into a sobering tailspin, because I had to face the possibility that I was trying all of these different ventures because I didn't believe that I had what it took to be extremely successful as a motivational speaker and author. That night when I went home, I thought to myself, could he be right? Am I a mile wide and an inch deep, or am I simply a young up-and-coming entrepreneur? Either way, he got me to thinking.

I did an assessment of everything that I was involved in. That night I made a spreadsheet showing all the time, money, and effort that I was putting toward each of my ventures. I had to admit my dad was right. I was all over the place. I was using my dream to fund several nightmares. It seems even then I was in a state of *survival mode*. After that reality check, it became clear for me, it was time to put an end to the madness. Surprisingly, it was really easy for me to shut everything down. I thought that I was going to have a lot of internal struggle with the idea, but the reality was I was wasting time, money, and effort. The moment I placed the last box of chocolates on the curb, I felt a huge sense of relief. Now it was time to focus 100% of my time, effort, and energy on becoming the best motivational speaker and author that I could possibly be.

CHAPTER 16

From *Gucci* to
GERBER

*"Without pain and sacrifice, we will never
have anything worth having."*

-JONATHAN EDISON

Little did I know a chance meeting would lead to an entirely different lifestyle than the one I had become so accustomed to. In the summer of 2006, I was scheduled to speak for Daimler Chrysler's African-American Leadership Retreat at the Daimler Chrysler headquarters. It was a typical corporate event that required me to deliver a 90-minute presentation to approximately 200 people, but unlike some other corporate events, this one happened to be local. I was excited, because that meant my dad could man the credit card machine and help with the product sales immediately following my presentation. I will never forget the feeling of pride and joy that came over me when we would show up at events together. Whenever I had a local event he almost always made sure he was available.

We showed up to the Daimler Chrysler headquarters an hour early wearing custom tailored suits and matching Gucci loafers. (My father was an impeccable dresser, and he passed the torch to me.) We took our seats in the front row, and then it was show time. I made my way to the platform and I hit the audience with 90 minutes of my best stuff. Out of the corner of my eye I watched my dad watching me. I loved to make him laugh and see the look on his face when one of the jokes that I practiced on him went over really well. At the end of my presentation I received a standing ovation. That was my dad's cue to get the credit card machine fired up. I walked over to the table where the line was already beginning to form. People were eager to talk to me about the presentation and how it made them feel.

"Jonathan, that was fantastic!"

"Jonathan, that was great!"

"Jonathan, wow, do you speak at churches?"

About 10 minutes into the book signing, I noticed a strikingly beautiful young woman in line. She was about 5 '5, slender with beautiful brown eyes and a smile that lit up the room. It was love at first swipe.

"Hi, I would like to purchase the entire Unstoppable Kit," she said to my dad.

"Excellent, young lady, is there anything else I can get you?"

I was watching the interaction out of the corner of my eye. Was that a blush I saw high on her cheekbones? I was desperate to get this lovely girl's attention.

"No, that's it," she said with a huge smile. My dad was trying to swipe her card and help the next customer simultaneously, but his multitasking abilities weren't as honed as mine, so I decided to take over.

"Excuse me . . . are you attempting to purchase the entire kit?" I asked this beautiful young lady.

"Yes, I am, I gave your dad my credit card, but if it's faster, I can pay with cash," she replied. "By the way, my name is Karen."

I tried to think of something funny, anything at all, to say to this gorgeous woman.

"I like your style! Cash is king. That will be $99.00 please," I said. She paid and smiled as I packed her Unstoppable Kit.

My dad winked at me, because we both knew we were having a great sales day.

Once the day was done, we thanked everyone for their purchases and made our way to the parking lot. While backing the car out I was startled by my dad's voice.

"Look out! Stop the car!" he yelled.

I whipped around and realized I was about to plow right into a burgundy Dodge Charger passing directly behind us. Both of us slammed on the brakes. We were inches from plowing into each other—the other driver had to swerve up onto the curb. My Dad and I jumped out to see if the other driver was ok. When I approached, I noticed the driver had a familiar face and an Unstoppable Kit on her front seat. She rolled down the window and I heard my own voice blaring from her car speakers: "You are unstoppable!" WOW! I thought.

We locked eyes and laughed. I asked her if she was ok.

"Sure," she said.

"Why are you driving so fast in this parking lot? You almost killed us. What are you running away from? Are you stalking me?" I said jokingly.

"Boy, please. Who stalks a motivational speaker? I think you tried to hit me on purpose. All you had to do was ask for my number! You don't have to incapacitate me."

My dad and I just laughed. I asked for her number. After that chance encounter, Karen and I began dating. She intrigued me because we were complete opposites. She came from a very large family and I was an only child. She loved working for corporate enterprises, and I was an entrepreneur. Six months later, after many long dinners, movies, and a lot of getting to know one another, we were in love.

As my business and aspirations grew, she was right there to support me. Every idea, every crazy invention, every plan, you name it, she supported me—even when I decided to run for mayor of Detroit. I finalized my candidacy too late to make the primary ballot, but I was still in time to be a write-in candidate. I set out to be mayor without any political background, campaign funds, or even a campaign slogan, determined to prove people will value a person's work over what they say.

I ran (if I may say so) the most untraditional campaign in the history of politics. My first campaign tactic was to provide free passenger van shuttle service, coffee, and blankets to citizens throughout Detroit. I convinced several of my friends —

Kamal, D. Rogers, T. Burney, Earthel, Karl, and of course my wife — that this was a great idea. We drove around the city in 12 hour shifts in a 14 passenger van rented from Enterprise and met some really strange characters, but we also had a blast. One freezing cold night at around 12:30 a.m., we were out looking for people to give rides to. It didn't take long for the van to fill up. We were carrying about ten people when we spotted a guy walking and shivering. It seemed like he had been walking for quite some time. We pulled over to pick him up.

"Hey, big guy, can we give you a ride? Where are you going?"

He replied that he was headed to downtown Detroit, about 3 or 4 miles from our current location. He paused and looked through the window of the van.

"Are you dropping off these people first? Because I don't have time to wait!"

I laughed, because there he was walking in the bitter cold, and even after dropping everyone else off, we'd still probably beat him there if he kept walking. What was this guy thinking? But I replied, "Yes, sir, but we can get you downtown right after."

He looked in the van one more time and said, "No thanks, I'd rather walk."

We couldn't believe it! Who'd turn down a free ride in the middle of the winter in -12 degrees? But people are weird!

Our second strategy was to do a Shoveling for Seniors event. We set up an 800 number for senior citizens to call if they needed help shoveling their snow. Karen manned the phones, and they never stopped ringing. The funny thing was, when we arrived at some homes, a fully-grown man would answer the door and say, "Oh yeah, my grandmother told me to call you guys to shovel her snow." Really, captain lazy! We would thank them for their support and move on. But we did find several homes where senior citizens had no one to assist them with their snow removal. I remember Karen calling and saying "OK, some of these people are nuts. They act like they are paying for this service. I can't do this anymore. If you need me to, I will, but I'm tired of being yelled at."

When the election results came in we failed miserably, considering our effort. My biggest hurdles were trying to have people write my name in on the ballot and limited cash flow. I found out very quickly that it takes quite a bit of money to run a successful mayoral campaign in a large urban city.

Even so, even after all of the 800 calls, Karen didn't really mind. That's the part of her that I fell in love with, because she allowed me to be ME. Free to think, free to explore, free to fail, free to dream, free to risk, free to create, free to try, free to flop, free to win, free to cry, free to soar, and free to become the best Jonathan Edison possible. I will always love her for that from the depths of my soul.

On July 20, 2007, we welcomed Jonathan Edward Edison, Jr.

to the planet. My first son! When he was born I was so flooded with emotion I couldn't stop crying. I looked at him for the first time and I whispered, "Jonathan, I am going to be the best dad in the history of dads. I promise." I knew I had huge shoes to fill, but I also knew my dad had equipped me with everything I needed to keep my word.

With Jonathan Jr. came bills, bills, bills. When I tallied up the cost for the stroller, car seat, diapers, breast pump, clothes, and jars of Gerber, I looked at my feet and I knew I would have to say goodbye to my favorite Gucci loafers. But navigating this new role was a lot easier than I thought it would be. I thought that being a dad would mean giving up my identity and no longer enjoying my life. But I quickly found out being a dad was all about getting closer to the meaning of life and becoming a more caring and loving human being. I absolutely love being a father. I wouldn't trade it for the world.

Just as I was getting the hang of things, Karen told me, "I think we have another one on the way. It must have been that champagne I got you last month."

Are you serious? I thought. But I just laughed and said, "OK, well, I have something I want to tell you."

"Yes?"

"Close your eyes and I'll tell you," I teased.

"Boy, stop playing with me," she yelled. Then I got down on one knee and asked for her hand in marriage.

"Where did you get this ring from? This is wayyyyyyyyyy too much!" she shouted. I laughed.

"Is that a yes?"

"Yes!"

In the beginning I wasn't sure how all of this was going to play out. Now we had a "just-add-water" family of five, including Karen's young son Joshua, from her first marriage. Instead of my speaking income and product sales going toward the things I liked, it went to groceries, medicine, child care, extra-curricular classes, Little League, groceries, day camps, snacks, more groceries, gas, baby gear, even more groceries, shoes, clothes and, lastly, groceries. I thought I was going to lose my mind — I never slept more than three hours for those first three years. I even made the ultimate sacrifice and purchased a used car with over 150,000 miles on it so I wouldn't have the burden of a big car payment — not like my friends, who drove huge SUVs and sporty new rides.

I never knew having a family came with so much leadership and financial responsibility. In my single days I came and went as I pleased and for the most part, I lived without a budget. I shopped whenever I felt like it, ate out all the time at expensive restaurants and drove a luxury sedan. I guess what brought it all home for me was one day checking out at the grocery store. The clerk said, "That will be $459.00." My jaw dropped. I had never had a grocery bill over $100 before.

As I've grown as a person and a father, I have learned that the measure of a real man is not in the car he drives, the clothes he wears, or the people who scream his name. The measure of a real man lies in his ability to lead, guide, and protect his family at all costs. I thought I was going to miss my single, free life. But I don't miss one bit of it. I love being a leader, husband, dad, and businessman. Yes, there have been quite a few sacrifices along the way and a lot less shopping for myself, but I wouldn't trade my family and what I have for a hundred pairs of Gucci loafers. When Karen and I started our family, I was totally lost, with no emotional focus or purpose. But now I've truly found myself as the leader of the Edison clan.

CHAPTER 17

Reconnecting with
DAD

"Invisible Threads are the strongest ties."

-FRIEDRICH NIETZSCHE

At age 20, I had been estranged from my dad for more than six years. My girlfriend at the time, Carla, picked me up to have lunch in the Mexican Village one afternoon and the absolutely unexpected happened. We happened to be driving near my dad's house and she asked me a question that has directly and profoundly impacted my life more than anything else:

"John, doesn't your dad live a few minutes from here? You should go by and see him."

At first I shrugged it off, but deep inside I missed talking to him. After our big fallout and my move, all I could remember was the good times we had and the things he taught me when I was a kid. When I was nine, he noticed I enjoyed sports, but I was kind of skinny for my age. So he bought me a weight set from K-Mart. After several months of pumping iron and building my body, I decided I was ready to deadlift the entire 110-lb set over my head. Well, just seconds into my Olympic weightlifting career, I lost control of the weights, and I fell sideways—right out of the second story window of my bedroom. Glass went flying everywhere. Fortunately I was OK, and when I brushed myself off and looked up, there my Dad was looking down at me out of the frame of the broken window.

"Boy, who do you think you are, Mr. T? Breaking out windows and jumping from two stories up."

We both burst into laughter, and that became the "go to" story shared with all new visitors to my house for the next ten months.

"Hey, would you like something to drink? By the way, John fell out of his bedroom window with 110lbs of weights, trying to play Mr. T."

This and other memories like it ran through my mind as I considered Carla's suggestion. Impulsively, I decided to take her up on her offer. After lunch I told her to swing by there. When we pulled up to his house, I was nervous. I didn't know how he was going to respond. I was afraid that he wouldn't answer the door or just reject me all together. I suppose my greatest fear was being dismissed by him again. My heart was racing and my hands were sweaty as I walked up on the porch. The memories of our argument and of me dragging my mattress out of the front door returned in an unwelcome flood. I hesitated and almost aborted the mission. Back in the car, Carla smiled and yelled, "ring the bell, boy, and stop being a chicken!"

I turned around and rang the bell.

Ding-dong.

Seconds later my little brother Demetrius appeared at the door. "Daddy, John is here," he yelled.

A few moments later my father appeared in the doorway. He was wearing a silly black T-shirt that read "Don't You Love ME?"

I couldn't help but say under my breath, "Yes, I do, very much."

I followed him inside and sat down at the kitchen table.

"Are you hungry?" he asked.

I had just eaten a huge Mexican feast. I wasn't hungry at all.

"Yes, sir, I am," I said, with as much excitement as I could muster. I wasn't hungry for food, but I was hungry for love, the type of love only a father and son can share. I watched as he made the gravy for the mashed potatoes. It was the same recipe he taught me when I was six. My dad loved cooking, and he passed that love down to all of his children.

After about 20 minutes of waiting outside the house, Carla knocked on the door. I told my dad I would be right back. He nodded and continued stirring the gravy. I took Carla out onto the front porch, and she asked me close to a million questions in one breath.

"So what's going on, how is it, what are you guys doing, what did he say, are you staying? What's up, tell me tell me tell me!"

I laughed. "Girl, calm down! I can't answer all of these questions at once. I'll fill you in later. For now, my dad and I are about to have dinner. We'll see where it goes."

She was so happy for me. She heard me talk about him all the time, but knew I had never gathered the courage to reach out to him. I pulled her close and gave her a big kiss. "Thank you for bringing me."

She took her keys out of her purse, smiled, and whispered, "I told you so."

Now, I don't enjoy hearing I told you so, but in this case I was thrilled to make an exception.

From that day on my father and I were like old friends. We talked on the phone all the time, sometimes for more than four hours a day, and if we weren't on the phone I was at his place having dinner. And if we weren't having dinner we just sat and watched television together for hours. We were inseparable. For the next decade my dad became my motivator, life-coach, confidant, priest, sounding board, voice of reason, protector, and benefactor. I didn't make any major decisions in my life without first consulting my father. Jobs, girlfriends, trips, clothes, vehicles, investments, you name it, I ran it by him first. I didn't always follow his advice, but I always considered it before I made a final decision. It might have seemed a little extreme to some people, but my father had traveled the world, served in the Army, and ran several successful businesses. He opened a very popular bar and hotel called Lucky's in 1968 with the money he saved from four years of military pay. When he opened the bar, he ran a contest encouraging the patrons to take a photo of him every day. He promised not to wear the same outfit for an entire calendar year, and if he did, drinks were on the house for a whole month. Well, when the word got out about that deal, my dad became a fashion legend. He eventually sold the bar, but his reputation stayed intact. He retired comfortably at 50. Now I thought, *who better to listen to?* My coworkers? I didn't have any. My friends? Most of my friends were idiots making bad decisions and going nowhere fast. Meanwhile, I had someone in my corner that would go to bat for me under any circumstances, and talk to me about anything — no topic was off limits. My dad was my BFF way before most people knew what the term even meant.

After our reconciliation, I gave my father a themed birthday party every year to celebrate my admiration for him. The first couple of years were pretty simple. I did a Mexican theme and a backyard '70s BBQ. But as the years went on, my ideas became more elaborate.

For his 70th birthday in 2010, I threw the biggest and the best party my father ever had the opportunity to enjoy. I themed the party completely 007 style, like James Bond, from the cake to the champagne glasses down to the required attire for the evening, which was black and white cocktail wear. I rented out the top floor of the Atheneum Hotel, which is Detroit's premier hotel, with marble bathrooms and fantastic city views. While the partygoers arrived, I drove my dad around downtown Detroit with one of the best photographers in the city. We drank champagne, smoked expensive cigars, and toasted to life at the Spirit of Detroit statue, the Joe Louis Fist, and the Hazen S. Pingree monument. But the real party began when we pulled into the Atheneum. Two beautiful Bond Girls escorted him to the top level of the hotel. Inside the Senator, Governor, and Presidential suites, fifty or sixty of our closest friends and family members waited to surprise him. Just before he opened the door, he turned back to look at me.

"Thank you," he whispered.

Surprise!!!!!!!!!!!!!!!!!!!!!!!!!

The music began and the party got underway. Everyone was having a blast, my dad was overjoyed (he loved the spotlight), and I had pulled off one of the best surprise parties in history. About an hour into the night someone suggested we turn down the music and make time for a few words. *A toast – great idea,* I thought. I raised my glass.

"Ladies and gentleman, if I can have your attention: First of all, I want to thank all you for being here and participating in tonight's joyous occasion. Some of you have asked me why I would go to such great lengths just to have a party. Well, the answer is simple. This man standing to my left is the best man I know. He motivates me, he inspires me, he challenges me, and he is the best father a son could ask for. So I decided the best way to thank him is to show him how much I love him while he's alive to enjoy it. I know most of us in the room like to throw elaborate funerals for the people that we love, so I decided to do it in reverse!

Please raise your glass for the man of the hour, my father, Larry Edward Edison."

When I finished, a lot of people took out their cell phones and called their own parents. It was one of the best moments I've ever experienced. As the night came to an end I thought again about all the good times my Dad and I had shared, and about how this night was another memory to add to the list of good times.

Little did I know this would be our final party together on Earth.

JONATHAN EDISON

CHAPTER 18

In the
HOSPITAL

*"Life and death are one thread, the same
line viewed from both sides."*

-LAO TZU

The following year my dad seemed a little shaky from time to time, and he began having some minor health complications. When I took the kids over to visit he would tell me he felt great, he was just having some shortness of breath lately.

"Yeah, I'm not as spry as I used to be, but I still don't need Viagra." He joked.

It didn't seem really serious, but I found out he was experiencing chest pains and sneaking to the doctor to seek treatment. I knew behind the jokes and the quick wit, my father feared he would die like his mother at age 71. Even though my grandmother died from breast cancer, she suffered from a weak heart and was on medication for as long as I can remember. On February 5, 2011, a call came in. It was my little brother Demetrius.

"John, you need to meet us at the hospital. Pops is not doing so good."

I asked him what was going on, but he was too distraught to talk about it, so I just jumped in my car and drove to Harper Hospital in downtown Detroit where he was being treated. When I arrived at the hospital, my stepmother Tanzella was standing in the lobby in tears. She explained the night before my dad complained of shortness of breath and then began sweating and clutching at his chest. She decided to take him to the 24-hour emergency room, but when my dad's face began to turn blue and he lost consciousness, she realized she needed to get him to a hospital. When they arrived at the hospital he was in bad shape. The emergency unit on duty quickly cut all of his clothes off, turned him upside down and began treating him for a heart attack.

We all waited in fear as the minutes turned into hours. Five hours later the nurse came down and gave us the news.

"Hi, everyone. Mr. Edison suffered a severe heart attack, but he is stable. However, he is going to require surgery if he's going to live. You can go in and see him now but we need to make a decision on the surgery soon."

We joined my dad in his hospital room, which was full of strange, somber energy. It was hard for me to see my dad weak and in crisis like he was. Soon after the doctor came in and gave us an update.

"Mr. Edison, you have four blocked arteries and an additional fifth semi-blocked artery. If you want to live to see your 90th birthday, you have to have surgery within the next 48 hours."

When my dad heard that news he went into a complete panic.

"I don't need surgery; all I need is a cold Pepsi, some fresh air, and a good bowl of soup!" I knew for the first time in probably a very long time my dad was terrified and felt completely helpless.

The next morning we all reconvened at the hospital to meet with the surgeon and the attending doctor. My dad had calmed down a little, but he still was not convinced surgery was the best course of action. My dad was old school, and he needed proof everything was going to be fine. I took out my iPad and pulled up the stats on the surgeon for my father to see. "Dad, look. He's the best surgeon in the region at this surgery, and as a matter of a fact, he's the surgeon that teaches other surgeons how to perform this procedure. He doesn't have any outstanding malpractice lawsuits and he graduated at the top of his class. OK?!" My father was a stubborn old boy, but after my vetting, he knew he was in good hands. He agreed to have the surgery the following morning.

That was a long night of prayer for me. I asked God to extend my father's life so that he could have the opportunity to enjoy his grandkids. I was so proud to take them over to his house and show them off. He loved playing with them and he especially loved cooking for them. The next morning the entire family showed up to the hospital at 6:00 a.m. — me, Tanzella, Demetrius, and my younger sister. We tried to keep the energy high while we waited for the surgical staff to take my dad to the operating room. Tanzella and my siblings were doing their best to stay positive, but they were so worried, it was hard for them to keep from crying. When I felt the energy dropping to an all-time low in the room I decided I had to do something. I had read research suggesting that it was dangerous to send a patient into surgery while they were sad, depressed, or upset. So I went into my best Richard Pryor "All-Time King of Comedy" routine. My dad loved Richard Pryor and owned all of his albums. I used to sneak off and listen to them, and because my memory was so good, I was able to commit hours and hours of Richard Pryor material to memory. I was even able to do the voice and sound almost just like him. I gave my dad, the nurses, and my dad's roommate Mr. Jenkins a 20-minute impromptu show featuring *"Mud Bone,"* and I killed it. I've heard people talk about channeling the energy and spirit of people they admire, and for the first time in my life, I actually experienced that phenomenon for myself. For twenty minutes in that hospital room I became Richard Pryor -Live on Sunset Strip.

"Mr. Edison, it's time," said the nurse. My dad got up on the table, still laughing from the show, and then he was on his way. We all followed him to the elevator and reassured him we would see him in a few hours.

"Ok, I will see you guys in a little while," my dad said, and then he burst into tears. That's when I knew for sure he was terrified. I didn't know how to react. The little boy in me only knew him as a strong black man, a hero, tough guy, motivator, and optimist. I mean, this was the same guy that was shot in the stomach twice when two assailants tried to rob him outside of his bar and drove *himself* to the hospital. As the elevator doors closed, I looked at my reflection in the shiny metal and I saw myself at age five again, watching my parents fight with tears streaming down my face, wondering, how could Superman be afraid?

I knew there was nothing I could do in the operating room, but I could do plenty outside of it by praying for a successful surgery. So I excused myself and I took the long walk back to my car. I sat and prayed for 3 hours straight. Once I felt I was getting on God's nerves I joined everyone back in the waiting area.

The surgery took almost nine hours, but it was a success. Even so, my dad's recovery was difficult. He had to be placed on a ventilator for several days and spent another week in the intensive care unit. His medications were making him sick, his feet were swollen, and his blood pressure was very low. Something wasn't right, and the doctors couldn't figure it out. My dad ended up spending another three weeks in the hospital, and after a while he seemed to be giving up. He couldn't shave, because he was on blood thinners, he couldn't eat what he wanted, and most importantly (to him), he couldn't sleep in his own bed. I constantly wondered what I could do to speed up his recovery and to get him to see his compelling future. Then I got it. I went and placed all of the pictures from his 70th birthday party into an album so he could see the real Larry Edward Edison. I took that album up to his room the very next morning.

"Dad, this is the real you. Now quit fooling around, stop feeling sorry for yourself and get better." I yelled. I had never spoken to my father in that tone before, but I knew that's what he needed to hear. He started flipping through the photos and looking at himself, clean shaven in a beautiful black and white tuxedo. A spark set off in his eye. Over the next 48 hours everyone on my dad's floor of the hospital saw that album. Everyone knew he was a handsome, confident, strong and proud man, and that made him feel amazing. When I went back Friday, 2 days later,

he looked 20 years younger. He was talkative, laughing, joking, and ready to get out of that hospital. One week later, my dad was finally released and he felt great. A month later he was doing even better. He was eating what he liked to eat, and he was even able to go out and get a haircut and a shave. I couldn't be happier, because his grandbabies were dying to see him. Week after week they kept asking, "When can we see Paw Paw? Is he OK now?"

On Saturday, April 16, 2011 I took my 2-year-old baby girl Ava over to see her Paw Paw. That afternoon they played, talked, and had lunch together. It was the perfect day. The Monday, Tuesday, and Wednesday of the following week, I was on a speaking trip in Kentucky. I called my dad from the road like I always did, and he seemed to be in great spirits. But that Thursday I received a call from my brother in the middle of the night.

"John, Dad is sick, he's throwing up blood and he can't swallow. You need to get to the hospital." I immediately put an emergency call in to God.

"God, what's going on? I thought we took care of this already." I had prayed so much over the last two months, God and I were texting back and forth.

At the hospital I joined my family in the waiting room, where we waited to speak with a nurse.

"I have good news and bad news." Coming from a medical professional, this really means all of the news is terrible. This isn't a freaking Buick we are talking about.

"Mr. Edison seems to have a blockage in his lower intestine that was caused by the gunshot wound he suffered close to over 50 years ago. He could have another surgical procedure to remove the blockage, but there is a 95 percent chance he would have to wear a colostomy bag for the rest of his life." We were in shock.

"Ma'am, are you kidding?"

"No. This is very rare and very unusual, but this is the diagnosis." How could this be? My dad survived open-heart surgery, only to be threatened by this fifty-year-old wound? My dad's meticulousness and attention to detail would not take well to wearing a colostomy bag. I knew this was going to require a lot of convincing.

At the end of the day I was able to go up and see him, but he didn't look good. His room had that strange feeling again, as if the Angel of Death was lurking in the shadows.

I tiptoed slowly over to his bed, not wanting to disturb him.

"Hey, Dad, how do you feel?" I whispered.

"Aw man, I'm thirsty, I'm so thirsty." He whispered back in a very low voice.

"I'll get you something to drink."

"Is that water in your cup? Bring it over here so I can have a drink." I walked around to the right side of the bed with the styrofoam cup and he took a couple of shallow sips.

"I'm so thirsty. They won't let me eat or drink. I'm so thirsty." He kept whispering.

A few minutes later he drifted off to sleep. I sat back down next to his bed, barely controlling my emotions. Angry tears rolled down my face, in my head, I screamed at God. *God, DO SOMETHING. Because he doesn't deserve this.*

As he slept, the memories of our time together unspooled like a film through my mind. I sat there for three hours, sometimes chuckling, sometimes crying, sometimes gasping for air, as this movie of memories played on. I remembered how he bought me my first bike and let me follow him five miles home while he drove ahead with his hazard lights on. (Good times) I remembered when I was five, I accidentally set his king-size bed on fire. (Really, it was an accident!) I had been playing with my favorite ball in my dad's bedroom. It bounced off the wall and rolled under his bed. I got down on my hands and knees and tried my best to reach it but I couldn't. It was hard to see where it was, so I decided to get a light for some help. I grabbed a lighter that was nearby, scooted underneath the bed, flicked it on, and jackpot! I found my ball. Little did I know that light from a lighter under a king-size mattress meant FIRE.

The funny thing was that I didn't panic. I saw the smoke, walked into the kitchen, and grabbed my favorite cup from the sink. I filled it up and went back into my dad's room, got down on my hands and knees, reached under the bed, and doused the blaze. Then I calmly went back into the kitchen and filled up the cup over and over again.

After the 5th or 6th time my grandmother became suspicious and asked what I was doing.

"Oh, I'm putting out the fire in Daddy's room," I said, calm as could be. The next thing I know my dad sprang from his seat into the bedroom and yelled, *Call the fire department! This boy is trying to burn the house down!* Within 10 minutes the fire department was there. They put out the blaze and took away the ruined mattress. Surprisingly, I didn't get a whopping, but I never touched a cigarette lighter after that!

I was still "watching" the movie of our lives when I felt a tap on the shoulder. It was Tanzella.

"John, you can go. I'll sit with him tonight," she said. We didn't say much beyond that. We were both so sad. I gathered up my things, drove home, and prayed again, *Lord, take this pain away from Dad and bring him back to his old self, please, God, I beg of you.*

I didn't sleep well that night. I was really worried that my dad would refuse to have the surgery. I had planned to take the late afternoon shift and sit with him until dinner the next day at 4:00 p.m., but at 2 p.m. my brother called. He was nearly screaming.

"John, talk to Dad, he doesn't want to have the surgery and they're saying he will die if he doesn't go on the respirator, because his blood pressure is too low. . . talk to him, talk to him, please, talk to him!" My stepmother grabbed the phone.

"John, please, talk to your dad! Tell him he has a lot to live for, and he needs to take the air if he wants to live!" she yelled frantically, sobbing.

I heard Tanzella pass the phone and a lot of static and muffled noise in the background. In that moment it was like I was inside the *Matrix*. Everything around me froze in space. I heard my heart beating and felt the beads of sweat gathering on my forehead. Grief, panic, and hysteria attacked me all at once. I had given hundreds of speeches all over the world to hundreds of thousands of people, and at that moment, I didn't know what to say. The professional speaker was completely speechless and now little John-John "The Master of the Ghetto" was holding on the other line. After a few minutes, which seemed like years, I snapped back to myself, but before I could say a word I heard Dad's voice. I pulled over to the side of the road. I was attempting to gather my thoughts as fast as I could while dealing with the emotion of the moment, and I still hadn't said anything when he spoke.

"Hey, don't you worry about me, I've already talked to God and he wants me to come home. Here, Tanzella, take this phone. I'm going home now."

At 2:15 p.m. on April 25, 2011 my earthly father went home to be with his Heavenly Father.

CHAPTER19

Missing
YOU

*"Treasured in my heart you'll stay, until
we meet again someday."*

-ANON

That Friday at 1 p.m. we had his going-home celebration. The funeral home was packed; and I knew each person in attendance represented a life my dad had touched. During the family hour I had decided not to speak because my heart was so heavy. The minister opened the service up for remarks, and I didn't budge. Then as the final volunteer speaker left the podium, the minister extended the invitation to share something about my father one final time. I still sat anchored to that pew. Then, I swear, I felt something. It felt a like a huge pop to the back of head. My dad's presence was in the room and I knew that he wanted me to speak. I made eye contact with the minister.

"I would like to say something, if that's ok?" I took the podium and I looked out in the crowd. There were so many tears. My dad was all about having a good time and enjoying life—not teary faces and red eyes. I had to change the mood. At every speaking engagement I do, I run out of the room. Then I run back in, through the aisles, encouraging people to stand up and clap and go crazy. My dad always loved this part of my live speaking engagements. So I decided to honor him with it, one last time. I told the organist and the drummer to get ready. They looked stunned, but they agreed.

"Ok, ladies and gentlemen, if my father has had an impact on you and your life, on the count of three I want you to jump to your feet and shout and get excited." I ran out of the room.

One . . .
　　　Two. .
　　　　　Three!

I ran back in. The place erupted. It was magical. People clapped and shouted, and I think the organist and drummer held beat for a full 5 minutes. After everyone took their seats again, I shared a few short stories about my dad that made everyone laugh and cry. I wanted everyone to walk out of there remembering my father's motto, which was, "Live life to the fullest, because there is no guarantee you will be here tomorrow to enjoy it." I think I succeeded.

Just as the crowd was making its way out I noticed Tanzella walk over to my dad's casket to give him one last kiss before the attendants closed it. When I saw them reach for the lid, I looked away as quickly as I could. I couldn't bear to watch them close that casket on him. My brother Demetrius grabbed my hand, trembling.

"C'mon, bro, we have to get Dad and put him in the car." His voice shook. Then I took the longest and the most excruciating walk of my life up to the altar. It felt like I was walking in slow motion through quicksand with one thousand pound weights on my shoulders. The attendant handed me a pair of white gloves and I slowly and meticulously placed them on my hands, first my left and then my right. Once I had the gloves on I waited for a signal and then I received the nod from the head usher. Simultaneously, all of the pallbearers lifted my dad's casket and we turned toward the back door. The main attendant guided us out, and I was thankful, because underneath my oversized sunglasses my eyes were bloodshot and swollen from the constant crying fits I was having. I could hardly see where I was walking. As we walked toward the back door, I tried to pull myself together long enough to get him in the hearse safely. I didn't want the casket to slip out of my hands, so I locked step with the other pallbearers and channeled every ounce of strength into my right arm which was holding up my sweet, sweet prince. Once we secured my dad in the back of the waiting hearse, I tried to make my way through the crowd to the family limo that was waiting in the front of the church. I didn't make it. I collapsed right there in the parking lot, while clutching the glass of the hearse that my dad was in.

I went blank for several moments. I'm not sure who they were, but about seven guys helped me back to the family car out front. I think I had a panic attack, because I couldn't breathe and I was trembling and shaking in the back of the limo. The funeral home's nurse came and sat in the back of the limo with me. She took the gloves off my hands and folded them up neatly. She set them on the seat, and then she took my hands and placed them in hers. In a low and gentle voice she prayed I would find peace and comfort in the fact my father was in a better place. She prayed I would take joy in his being so proud of me for who I had become and what my future held. Somehow, after a few minutes of listening to her soothing voice, I was able to calm down enough to make the trip to the cemetery.

On the 15-minute ride over, it was completely silent in the back of the limo. I think my panic attack had scared everyone so much, they didn't want to say anything that would set me off again. No one looked at each other. It was just dead silence. Silence like in the middle of the night when the entire world is still. As we pulled into the cemetery, I heard nothing but the Cadillac tires kicking up the gravel. Off in the distance the American flag blew in the wind, and two soldiers, immaculately dressed and poised like marble statues, stood straight and still at attention, waiting for my dad's arrival.

All of the cars slowly and quietly made their way to the site. It was one of the most beautiful and glorious things that I had ever seen besides the birth of my babies. As I exited the car, I could hear my dad's voice saying in my head, "Now this is how you make an entrance." This was my dad's final moment in the spotlight. He always loved his curtain call, and this was the last party he and I would attend together. I was so thankful that my stepmother and siblings entrusted me with the task of selecting my dad's final ensemble. I chose his favorite dark blue double-breasted suit, triple white twill dress shirt, matching white tie and a white pocket square. Although, the funeral home said that shoes weren't necessary. I couldn't let him approach Peter's gates without his favorite blue suede Gucci loafers.

Now it was time for the moment of truth. As the attendants and the pallbearers removed my dad's casket from the hearse and placed it on the stand, the two soldiers prepared to perform the traditional song played at all military funerals, Taps. This is the song the entire United States military views as the most appropriate and touching part of a military funeral. Traditionally, the song is played on a small bugle accompanied by a small snare drum.

As the wind blew in from the south on this beautiful April afternoon, I watched as the soldiers did their best to secure a beautiful American flag across my dad's casket. Once they had the flag secured, both soldiers kneeled down stealth-like and picked up their instruments. A mournful sound erupted from the soldier's trumpet .The sad, measured melody threw me into an emotional tailspin. The second soldier beat the drum.

Ddddun...tap tap tap....ddddun...tap tap tap....dddddun....tap tap tap...ddddun...tap tap tap.

For three minutes, I let out the loudest pain-riddled bellow. You could have heard from a mile away. The sound resembled the pain and anguish of a mother bear in the wilderness that has found one of her cubs dead.

Noooooooooooooooooooooooooooooooo......... I cried out intensely.

My legs gave way underneath me. Several people did their best to try and hold me up. But the earth tilted off its axis and I felt my heart beating through my chest. I had tried to record the performance of "Taps" on my cell phone so I could have it forever, but I dropped it and crushed it under my feet as I staggered to the side. My emotions were overpowering. This was it. This was final. No more dinners. No more funny stories. No more just sitting and watching TV. No more visits. No more parties. No more advice. No more opinions. No more adventures. No more questions. No more answers. No more love. No more life and no more Dad.

The soldiers performed the folding of the flag ceremony and that made it even worse. I let out another uncontrollable bellow.

Noooooooooooooooooooooooooooooooooooooooooooooooooooo . . . .

I screamed with tears streaming down my face.

In dead silence, wearing their spotless white gloves, the soldiers carefully and methodically folded my dad's flag and then presented it to my stepmother. I had never witnessed anything so sad before. When the soldiers saluted our family and turned about-face, I lost it again. The tears streamed down my face like someone had turned on a faucet. My hands were numb and my head was pounding. I tried to gather myself to walk back to the car. Just then the unexpected happened, Tanzella came up behind me and placed her hand on my shoulder.

"John, I know this is breaking your heart. He was your best friend, and I know how much he meant to you. Please take his flag." I couldn't see her or the flag very clearly through my tears.

"Thank you," I whispered softly. "I really appreciate this."

I let her place the flag in my right arm while I hugged her with my left. Then I collapsed in the family car and went into a rage. I couldn't believe he was gone.

As we drove away all I could do was squeeze the flag as if it were his body. After about five minutes of squeezing with all my might, I decided that I needed to take it easy. I didn't want it to come undone. I was completely wiped out. I didn't have anything left. I was all cried out, my body was numb, my voice reduced to a faint whisper.

My sister organized a wake, but I only stayed for a little while. I was still too upset to eat, and only had a few small bites here and there. After a few minutes of watching people scarf down food and saying how sorry they were, I knew I had to get out of there. I said my final good-byes and made my way home. I was scheduled to speak at an event in Chicago the very next morning. I had thought about cancelling, but didn't. I knew that I would need something to occupy my mind, and sitting at home grieving would just make me feel worse. But now I wasn't sure. As I looked at my travel bag, trying to make the right decision, I could hear my dad's voice as clearly as if he was standing next to me. ***"Boy, you better pick that bag up and get your butt in that car and go get that money."*** I laughed, cried a bit more, and I got my butt in that car. I drove all night. While I drove, I was able to calm down, pray, and get myself into a place of peace. I talked to my dad the entire way. I thanked him for all he had taught me and done for me. When I arrived in Chicago five hours later, my heart was full.

It's amazing what comes into your mind when you calm down and get really quiet. Later that night my dad began to speak to me again, in the form of a memory we shared. All of his life my dad was a connoisseur of great speeches, books on tape, and inspirational quotes. One in particular that he shared with me many years ago that came flooding into my mind as I sat on the bed in my hotel room was by the famous General Douglas Mac Arthur:

"Old soldiers never die; they just fade away."

Dad, I'm missing you.

Life ain't always what it seems to be
Words can't express what you mean to me
Even though you're gone, we still a team
Through your family, I'll fulfill your dream.
In the future, can't wait to see
If you open up the gates for me
Reminisce some time, the night they took my friend
Try to black it out, but it plays again
When it's real, feelings hard to conceal
Can't imagine all the pain I feel
Give anything to hear half your breath
I know you're still living your life after death.

-PUFF DADDY

CHAPTER 20

Life *After*
DEATH

"Death smiles at us all, all a man can do is smile back."

-MARCUS AURELIUS

When I returned from Chicago, I had a ton of voicemails from people sharing their love and sympathy for my loss. My mother even called, asking if I wanted to have lunch and talk about my dad. I declined, because not only did I feel it was too soon, I felt it was highly inappropriate. She had never wanted to talk to me about anything else or expressed interest in anything happening in my life. I was in no mood to reminisce about the most painful day of my life, especially with her. I was focused on trying to cope and finding a way to continue my journey. Luckily, my wife was there for me every step of the way. She supported me through my dad's illness, the funeral, and the months of grief following, and I love her for that. She even gave her best shot at trying to hold me up during the funeral. But her 5'5" frame caved after a few seconds of my 230 lbs. leaning on her.

My kids' memories of my father's funeral were blurry, but they asked about him constantly. They wanted to know what he talked like, where he lived, what kind of car he drove, and what he liked to eat. I sat Jonathan Jr. and Ava down and I told them everything. I told them their Paw Paw was a great man that loved everyone. He was a business owner, a former Harlem Showboat, a philanthropist, a snorkeler, and a really great cook. Their eyes lit up. *"Dad, your dad was awesome—why didn't you save him?"* asked 3-year-old Ava.

I did my best to explain that her Paw Paw didn't need saving, because he wanted to go see God.

"Well, at least he could have waited for me!" she said with a very serious face!

"Sugar, it doesn't work like that, but I understand where you're coming from."

I was faced with leading this new tribe without the benefit of my father's guidance. How was I going to hold it together without his advice? Luckily, I still had business coming in, because my marketing juices were drained. I would show up to an event, turn it on, and fly home in a complete fog. Many times I would accidentally call him because I still had his number programmed in my phone. Sadness permeated my body, mind, and spirit every single day. But I never let my kids see me sad; I always looked happy for them, and I did everything humanly possible to make sure they felt loved.

The biggest reminder of why I work so hard to be a great dad was fast upon me: September 8, 2011, my birthday. For 16 years consecutively my father called me on my birthday at 6:05 p.m., the exact time I was born. And this was the first year I wouldn't hear him say, *"Hey, another year. How do you feel? How's life treating you? And what are you going to do bigger and better?"* My wife took me to dinner that evening, and I did my best to hold it together. But when my phone didn't ring, and I didn't see my dad's number on the caller ID, I didn't much feel like celebrating. I thought to myself, *this is crazy, I know he's not going to call,* but every fiber of my being ached to hear the phone ring.

I've heard time heals all things. But even after the time that has passed, my heart is still in pieces. I mourn my father more and more as time goes on. I'm not sure if the pain I feel will ever go away, but I'm taking small steps day by day to manage it. I've read books about handling grief, and I joined a support group for people who have lost close loved ones. But none of them were able to fill in the gaping hole in my heart.

One year after my father's passing, my speaking business was doing OK, but I felt myself slipping into a real funk. I wasn't growing, and I definitely wasn't as focused as I should have been. So late one night—it was 3 a.m.—I went down to my home office and had a long conversation with my dad. I stared directly at his picture and talked to him as if he was sitting right in front of me.

In my home office I had set up a collage of pictures of him and hung his flag behind my desk, so I could always experience his energy.

"Pops, what do you think I should do? I want to take my business to the next level, but I feel stuck. What should I do?" I said, staring directly at his image.

Well, he came through yet again, because that night he set the wheels in motion for me to meet an angel.

While I was talking with my father, I doodled on a legal pad. I wrote down one question that has changed my life dramatically. The question is deceptively simple, but complex when you actually take the time to appreciate it. It's a question that has revolutionized my life. A question that is very easy to comprehend. A question that has made me a better human being. A question that has given me a renewed faith in God. A question that has virtually made me "UNSTOPPABLE" in life.

Are you ready for the question?

OK. Here it is....

One...
Two....
Three . . .

HOW CAN I DO THIS BETTER?

Or in other words...
how can you do what you do better?

No matter what it is...
You fill in the blank._____

I know what you're thinking, that's it? That's all? But allow me to explain. When I actually wrote this question down on paper, it forced me to assess where I was and where I wanted to be. I realized I had been too focused on my **ego** – **E**dging **G**od **O**ut. I had to remove my ego from the equation and make room for God.

That night I made a list of the top ten motivational speakers in my industry. These ten individuals represented what I wanted to be—respected, recognized, and battle-tested, successful in the vocation I loved. Once I made the list, I crafted an email sharing who I am, where I'm going, and how I thought they could assist me. I must have typed 25 or 30 different drafts of that email until I got it right. I even sent it to myself to see if I would respond to it before I sent it off. A week passed and I received two responses. One speaker's assistant called and told me my request was impossible. Well, the next week brought a response from my angel's executive director of 20 years, Teresa Biehl. Teresa's email would alter the course of not only my business, but my life.

Hi Jonathan,
Connie Podesta is out on a speaking tour for the next 3 weeks, but when she returns, she promises to give you a call.

Teresa

Connie is a 25-year veteran of the speaking industry and has created a multimillion dollar speaking enterprise. She is one of the most respected keynote speakers on the circuit. After a few weeks went by, I honestly forgot about her promise. But headed to the airport one day on my way home from an engagement in Illinois, a Texas area code flashed on my caller ID. I picked up.

"Hi, may I speak with Jonathan? This is Connie Podesta."

I was shocked. I couldn't believe it. I yelled, "Oh my God, this is Connie Podesta . . . is this really Connie Podesta? Oh my God. This is Connie Podesta!"

She just laughed and laughed. Then she said, "I know who I am, Jonathan, now let's see what I can do to help you with your business."

I turned the car around as fast as I could and pulled into a Steak and Shake parking lot in Springfield, Illinois. I just had one question. You know what it is by now.

"Connie, how can I make my business better?"

Well, she talked for the next three hours. I took notes on everything I had in the car — my legal pad, napkins, my forearm, the dashboard, and the fast food wrappers on the floor. It was like I was trying to get a drink from a fire hose going full blast! When the call ended, my right ear was smoking from the heat of what I had taken in. My head was spinning and my heart was pumping. My prayers had been answered—finally, someone gave me really good advice on how to go to the next level. I made it to the airport at last, and when it was time to board, *bing!* A three-page email from Connie Podesta showed up in my inbox. This lady was a dynamo.

I read her email on the plane. She gave me more instructions on creating a profitable, well-run business. She talked about changing my website, adding new programs, and offering a wider variety of products and services. Most professional speakers operate out of a scarcity mentality. Competition is so fierce in our business that very few speakers share their expertise and knowledge. I was overjoyed one of the top speakers on the circuit was willing to coach me and guide me to the next level. The only weird thing was, she wanted me to change my style of dress. She suggested that I try a blue blazer, open collared shirt and khaki pants, and I thought no way! I was used to wearing a single or double breasted suit with a tie, pocket square, and cufflinks. But everything else that she suggested was spot on. (SMILING…sorry, Connie).

When my plane touched down I couldn't wait to get back to my office so I could get to work. Over the next month we talked every day, sometimes two or three times a day. After I started implementing all of her strategies, I told her it was time for us to meet in person. She agreed.

"Jonathan, how about you come to Dallas and meet with me at my home? We can fly over to Austin and you can see me speak, and then we can return to Dallas and spend another day together." I couldn't believe that this very busy, incredibly successful woman was willing to give me this level of exposure into her world. It was a dream come true. I flew to Dallas, Texas the following Thursday. I met Connie at her beautiful home in Dallas, Texas, which was full of custom-designed furniture, fine art, and décor straight out of an interior design magazine. We sat out by the pool, and that's when the teaching began.

For the next four hours Connie talked to me about the three main challenges in the speaking business: how to sell myself as a speaker, how to drive more traffic to my website, and how to set my speaking career up for long-term success. I was taking notes so fast, my pen was smoking and the paper was practically on fire. When my hand got tired, I recorded her on my phone, so I could review her advice later. After the four-hour marathon, we decided it was time to eat dinner and shut down for the night.

Her driver took me to my hotel, but once I made it up to my room I couldn't sleep. Too many thoughts, too many ideas, too much to digest, too much to do to sleep. My mind was racing with ways to change my business and make it better, thoughts on how to secure more bookings and ideas of what resources I needed to increase my operation. The next morning her driver picked me up, and we headed together to Austin, Texas. We didn't waste a second—she talked to me during the drive, through security and boarding, and then for the entire duration of the flight to Austin. In Austin there was a limo waiting to pick us up and guess what, we talked the entire ride over to the hotel. I had never met anyone who loved to talk as much as I did, and it was awesome! This lady I had never met before was speaking my language. What a breath of fresh air she was at this critical and pivotal time in my life! I knew my dad had something to do with setting this up. That night we met at the bar for dinner, and we went at it again for the entire meal. When we came up for air it was 2:15 a.m.

Early the next morning we met at Starbucks and then it was

time to make our way up to the ballroom. Five-hundred Texas bankers were waiting for her keynote address. Connie hit the stage and she shifted into high gear. She gave her signature talk on *"How to Stand Out from the Crowd."* She didn't just dazzle the audience, she took over the room with her poise and humor. I immediately noticed she was a gifted comedian, because for the first fifteen minutes she had the room in stitches. Then she smoothly transitioned into getting the audience more involved by having volunteers join her on stage. I could see why she commanded the big bucks in our industry. Once she was finished, the audience gave her a five-minute standing ovation. Immediately following her presentation several people approached her to ask about her availability for other events. I stood there with my mouth wide open the entire time, in awe of what she had just done. She was so eloquent, so gracious, the consummate entrepreneur and business professional. Walking back to my hotel room, all I could think was how surreal this moment was. Here I was, a complete stranger, tagging along with one of the top speakers in my industry. *Lord, if I'm dreaming, please don't wake me up.*

That night over drinks we talked about my story, my stage presence, and my delivery. What she shared with me that night really changed my business. First of all, I had never thought of myself as a salesman, I only thought of myself as a speaker. But according to Connie, that's the mistake most speakers make. She showed me that I needed to be a better salesman in order to secure events with conference planners. She walked me through a process she has used for 10 years that allows her to stay on top of the industry. After the one-hour training she decided that we needed to do a live role-play.

"Role-play!" I yelled. I didn't like the sound of that.

Yes, Jonathan, a role-play . . .I'm going to call your phone, and I'm going to pretend to be the meeting planner and you are going to sell me on you and why I should hire you."

It felt a little weird, because I had never role played on the phone before, but after about an hour or so I started to feel a little more comfortable. This shifted my paradigm completely about what my role was as a professional speaker and business owner. She also said my marketing strategy was in desperate need of an overhaul. We went through my website page by page and began discussing what I needed to do to make it pop. This was mind blowing for me, because I assumed that I had a pretty great website, but she taught me how to look at my site from a meeting planner's perspective. She showed me that my marketing and the content of my web pages were all highlighting me, and not focused on solving the business problems of the meeting planners—like increasing sales, becoming better leaders, or increasing productivity.

Our last day back in Dallas we spent ripping and running across the metro area. We made our last stop at Connie's office to meet up with the mystery woman, Teresa. Teresa, Connie, and I all laughed and talked for hours and that's when it happened. "Jonathan, what would you think about coming on board with us? Of course you would keep your business separate, but would you consider being a part of our family and having your headquarters in Dallas, Texas?"

Are you kidding me?

"Yes, I'm in!" I said, with the biggest grin on my face.

My business and my life has never been the same. In one year, my business quadrupled in income. We raised my speaking fee three times in one year **(which is completely unheard of in the industry)**. I still don't know what possessed Connie to invite me into her inner circle, but I am so thankful she did. She doesn't know it, but since my dad's passing, she has become one of the most influential and inspiring people in my life. The time Connie and I have spent together over the last two years has changed my perspective in every area of life. I now run my business like a business and not a part-time hustle. I now make sure I plan ample time for family activities that allow us to grow together.

And honestly, for the first time in my life,
I don't feel like I'm in
Survival Mode.

Connie Podesta - You're the Best!
Love, Jonathan

CHAPTER 21

40 *Years* a
SURVIVOR

"I'm a survivor, I'm not going to give up,
I'm going to work harder"

-BEYONCÉ

I was born on September 8, 1973. In 2013, as I celebrated my 40th birthday, I realized my journey had also begun exactly 40 years ago. I remember a time in my life when I didn't think I would make it to be fifteen. Now, as I look back on my journey, I can honestly say I'm thankful just to be alive and well. Life hasn't been all basketball and pancakes, but it has provided me with tremendous lessons.

I cherish each and every challenge because collectively, they have made me into a better father, husband, businessman, and human being. As strange as this may sound, I wouldn't want it any other way. I have no regrets, and I am sure the next chapter of my life will be filled with great adventure, love, joy, twists, turns, and extraordinary accomplishments. I don't know what the future holds, but I do know I am battle tested and well trained to handle what comes my way. I'm reminded of one of my favorite historical figures, Frederick Bailey Douglas, who said, "Where there is no struggle, there is no progress."

Survival Mode for me has been a **real opportunity!** Without it, I would not be the man and human being I am today. I know you're thinking, "Jonathan, c'mon, you mean to tell me being in Survival Mode is a *good* thing?" Well, let's look at some of the benefits. It has forced me to be creative, vigilant, optimistic, imaginative, flexible, tough, strong, gracious, tenacious, diligent, and unrelenting. It has pushed me beyond my physical, mental, and spiritual limits. It has fueled my courage, so nothing on this planet can have power over me. Finally, it has driven me to explore, expand and engage in the gift of life! I call it a gift, because as long as you're living it keeps on giving — giving us love, challenges, pain, hurt, setbacks, mystery, stress, joy, happiness, defeat, ups, downs, great moments, birth, death, and my favorite, *UNCERTAINTY.*

Knowing this, I ask the most obvious question:

Is **SURVIVAL MODE** a *blessing* in disguise?

EPILOGUE

Dear reader:

I want to thank you for taking this journey with me. I really appreciate your support and love. Writing **Survival Mode** was a labor of love for me that ignited a montage of emotions within me. During the writing process it was simultaneously exciting, painful, heart-wrenching, sad, joyful, anxiety filled, and cathartic. I set out to pour my soul onto each and every page so that you could have the most enjoyable reading experience possible. It was very difficult to reduce 40 years of experiences into one literary work, but I really feel confident in the fact that I provided you with a very in depth detailed description of my journey and the challenges that I faced along the way. My hope is that you use my journey as a source of inspiration, motivation, and healing for your life. It's not an accident that you picked up this book and read it. It really means that you and I are kindred spirits navigating this *"thing"* that we call life together. On a deeper level I want to share with you that no matter what type of *"Survival Mode"* you're in... YOU ARE NOT ALONE!

My final message to you is one that I was inspired by in middle school from a local DJ who called himself "The Electrifying Mojo." For twenty years at the end of his 8pm -12pm broadcast he would always close it by saying the same thing.

> *"If you find yourself at the end of your rope;*
> *Tie a knot and keep hanging on."*

-ELECTRIFYING MOJO

My Granny CLORAINE M. TURNER
(My Heart)

Early Saturday morning - ME AND GRANNY

THE MCDONALD'S ON THE
EAST SIDE OF DETROIT
where my dad and I ate lunch on Saturday's

THE STREET I
GREW UP ON
before Chrysler relocated
our community

THE WAREHOUSE
that my mother and Donovan held me in

This is a photo of
MY AUNT'S HOUSE IN DETROIT

MY LIVING SPACE
that I paid $50 a month and half of the light bill for

THE BOX SPRING
spring that my dad allowed me to have
after I decided to leave his house

THIS WAS MY BLACK FOOTLOCKER
where I kept my clothes

CARLA D. STAMPS

An "Angel" that encouraged me, loved me, and pushed me to see a larger vision of myself. LOVE you always, Carla. Thank you!

OSBORN HIGHSCHOOL *graduation 1991*

WAYNE COUNTY COMMUNITY COLLEGE DEGREE

ME AND MY DAD,
the day I graduated from Wayne County Community College

WILKINS ELEMENTARY SCHOOL
MR. EDISON - KDGN. PM

1995   1996

My last semester of student teaching at
WILKINS ELEMENTARY SCHOOL

Spain School Students vs. Teachers Basketball Game
- MY BEST "LEBRON"

BACHELORS DEGREE
from Wayne State University

MASTERS DEGREE
from Wayne State University

JONATHAN EDISON

Me featured in the
MICHIGAN CHRONICLE
as the youngest assistant principal in
Detroit Public Schools' history at age 27

232

MEETING LES BROWN
*the World Renowned
Motivational Speaker*

MY FIRST PHOTO SHOOT
*for my new Motivational
Speaking Business*

OPENING NIGHT AT SWEET GEORGIA BROWN
(from left) My dad, Lavan Hawkins, Conrad Mallet,
yours truly, and Frank Taylor

MY LIFE SAVINGS
returned to me VOID

ANGIE AND I FEATURED IN
THE DETROIT NEWS
while attending the Cars and Stars event.
Courtesy of La Van Hawkins

This is what 1 MILLION DISH TOWELS *looks like*

235

When I met
MY WIFE KAREN

THE BIRTH OF AVA
with little JE

Ava and her PAW PAW

MY NEW YOUNG FAMILY

KAREN, MY MOTHER,
JONATHAN JR. AND AVA.
*This was my final attempt to reconcile
with her by inviting her over for dinner.*

BIG JE &
LITTLE JE
at Christmas

MY YOUNG FAMILY *getting ready for my dad's funeral*

My Last Gift to my Father
on his birthday

My Dad's Final Birthday Party

My Dad's Funeral.

My Dad's Flag

WALL OF FAME
in my office

*Standing
Head to Knee Pose
in* HAWAII

DELIVERING A KEYNOTE SPEECH
to over 1,400 people

A "SELL OUT" BOOK SIGNING
in the Bahamas after my morning Keynote speech

THE FUTURE LOOKS BRIGHT!
JE Jr. on the road with his dad

*I'm not sure what the future holds for me,
but I'm going to keep moving forward.*
NO MATTER WHAT!

*Studying for my
Finals at Harvard*
TO BE
CONTINUED

ADDITIONAL PRODUCTS

If you've enjoyed Survival Mode, check out these other thought-provoking, bestselling books by Jonathan Edison:

Survival Mode,
Also checkout Teacher and Student Editions

What's Your Motivation?

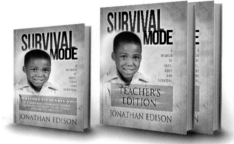

Transformational Leadership

The Parent Companion, Also available in Spanish and Hatian-Creole

Jo Jo - The 90 Day Motivator

If you would like to order any of these products in bulk please call Edison Speaks International **1-972-755-4231** for a SPECIAL DISCOUNT.

Please visit **www.shopjonathanedison.com**

GIVE A PAIR & GET A PAIR PROGRAM

At IRTS we are **giving away 50,000 pairs of socks**
to aid the homeless.

We are also collecting 50,000 pair of socks that will be donated
to the top 10 homeless shelters in America. Once you receive
your socks in the mail we are asking that you mail a pair of
gently used or new socks to the following address.

I'm Rocking These Socks
143 Cady Center Drive suite #165
Northville, MI 48167

PLEASE VISIT:
www.ImRockingTheseSocks.com

DONATE TODAY!

ACKNOWLEDGEMENTS

I would like to thank my family for supporting me and believing in me during this process. My wife Karen, my son Jonathan Jr., my baby girl Ava and my bonus son Josh. Everyone in the house knew that I was writing this book and they gave me the much needed space and time that was required for me to finish. I would like to thank Kendra Cagle for all of her hard work on this project. I would like to thank Cheryl Owens for her unbelievable effort and commitment. I would like to thank our trusted and most valuable "Baby Sitter" extraordinaire Akeema Richards. I would also like to thank Amber Shelby for her feedback and motivation. I would especially like to thank Ruth Curry (Editor) for her direction, guidance, and brutal honesty. The editing process for this project was a six-month grueling battle. But, in the end your steady hand and editing wisdom helped me give birth to a literary work that is positioned to inspire the masses. Without these individuals this project wouldn't be possible.

Finally, I would like to thank God for the creativity and the ability of expression that he granted me in the form of a gift that can be shared with the world.

Big "SHOUT OUTS" to the following businesses for allowing me to write, think and create in their space:
Starbucks, Hilton Hotels, Hyatt Hotels, Trump Hotels, Delta Airlines, American Airlines, US Airways, Duncan Doughnuts, Chuck E. Cheese and of course my absolute favorite "every airport along my journey that had free Wi-Fi."

SURVIVAL MODE

BOOK CLUB GUIDED QUESTIONS

For Discussion

1. What is your personal definition of Survival Mode?

2. Why do you think Jonathan's mother was so in love with Donovan?

3. Do you believe that Jonathan's father knew what was going on the entire time?

4. Why do you think Jonathan's grandmother decided to become his primary care giver?

5. Do you think that Jonathan's dad's heart was broken?

6. Why do you think Jonathan's mother decided to kidnap him?

7. Do you think Jonathan's 2nd grade teacher was fair in her assessment of Jonathan's future?

8. Do you think that Jonathan's father was being hard on him by making him peel those potatoes?

9. How do you think Jonathan felt when his grandmother passed away?

10. Why do you think Jonathan decided to trust Coach J?

11. Where do you think the turning point was for Jonathan?

12. In what ways do you think God had an impact on Jonathan's life?

13. Do you think Jonathan's father missed him as well?

14. How do you interpret Mrs. Edward's issue with Jonathan advancing in his studies?

15. Why do you think La Van Hawkins did what he did?

16. Do you feel that Jonathan's deep depression was warranted?

17. How do you interpret the "surge" of energy that Jonathan experienced during his speech for the police cadets?

18. Would you have still given the speech for the Michigan Horse Council?

19. Why do you think Jonathan failed so many times at so many different businesses?

20. How do you interpret Jonathan's "chance" meeting with Karen?

21. Why do you think Jonathan's father made the tough decision not to accept treatment at the hospital?

22. Jonathan writes in Chapter 19 that his father's death was too overwhelming. Why do you think Jonathan had such a tough time with his dad's death?

23. What impact did the question "How can I do this better?" have on Jonathan's life following his father's death?

24. In Chapter 21 Jonathan describes Survival Mode as an "opportunity." Do you believe that being in Survival Mode is an "opportunity?"

25. If you're currently in Survival Mode, has this book changed your perspective? If yes, then how?

A CONVERSATION WITH
JONATHAN EDISON

How is your relationship with your Mother today?

Currently, I don't have much of a relationship with my mother. I would like to, but it just seems impossible for us to get on the same page. I've tried on several occasions to reach out to her and show her that I still love her but all of my attempts have fallen short. Let me also say that my mother is an AMAZING person! She completed college and a nursing degree from one of the toughest institutions in the state. She also adopted my uncle's 2 girls and raised them like they were her own. When she received both girls they were addicted to crack and heroin and she nursed them both back to health. Now, both of them are in college and living very productive lives. When I think about my mother I often think about the story of Moses in the bible. Moses's mother's only job was to get him to the planet so that he could make an impact in the lives of other people. I feel that my mother's job was to get me here and it's my job to make a mark that cannot be erased.

Do you have any regrets?

Wow! That's a great question. I don't have any regrets, because when I look back over my life, I have to acknowledge the fact that I wouldn't be where I am if my life had played out any differently. One small change in the cycle would have disrupted everything. I'm actually thankful for every experience, every challenge, and every lesson. But I do feel like I could have done a better job at keeping up with some of my friends along the way. I guess that's why someone created Facebook.

Do you feel like you're out of Survival Mode?

I DO! Because for the first time in a long time I'm *clear* and *focused* on exactly what I want out of life. But, I'm not naïve enough to believe that life's challenges and Murphy's law are done with me by a long shot! I'm enjoying this journey called Life!

If someone is in *Survival Mode* what's the best way for them to get out?

I feel that the best way for someone to get out of *survival mode* is to stay active. Staying active keeps the mind and the imagination fluid. What challenges attempt to do is slow you down to a slow crawl until it becomes increasingly difficult for you to focus and execute. For example; if a person is thrown into *Survival Mode* because of a sudden divorce. I would recommend that the individual stay active, by writing out a 3 year plan that does not include that former spouse. It's hard to do when your heart is hurting and your emotions are raging, but it's necessary if you want to get out of *Survival Mode.*

Jonathan, as an "Inspirational Speaker" and "Success Strategist," who inspires you?

Great question...Great people that care about people inspire me. I have a vast list of individuals that fit that description, but there is one at the top of the list for me. Academy Award winning Actor and Director - "America's Leading Man" Denzel

Washington. Now let me share with you why I believe he's one of the most inspirational dudes on the planet!

Recently, Denzel was interviewed by GQ magazine when he turned 55. In the interview Denzel was asked about his success and *what the secret of success is.* I have to admit that his answer to these questions caught me totally off guard. Everyone has always known that he was an incredibly talented and gifted actor. And one handsome (YOU KNOW WHAT!) But, I was totally unaware of his deep spiritual conviction and his level of faith in God. Denzel shared with the interviewer that his secret to success (to paraphrase) was making sure that everyday when he opened his eyes and his feet hit the floor, that he would take his "favorite" thing or the thing that he needed the most to get out of the front door...coffee cup, keys, wallet, blow dryer-whatever it was...and he would throw it under the bed as far as he could. The interviewer looked puzzled and asked why would you do such a thing... and then Denzel with the eloquence of a great ing leading a tribe of millions said, *"I do that to ensure 2 things- #1 It ensures that I slow down in life and #2 It ensures that I start my day on my knees giving thanks to GOD for all of his incredible works, mercies and blessings."*

Now, if that doesn't inspire YOU, NOTHING WILL!

What types of groups do you often speak to as a motivational speaker?

I speak to a variety of different groups ranging from Fortune 500 companies, sales organizations, franchises, governmental groups, associations, health care organizations, real estate professionals and education schools, civic groups, and church organizations.

Who are some of your clients?
CORPORATE:

Aflac, Blue Cross and Blue Shield, Chase Bank, Colonial Life Insurance, Comerica Bank, CVS Pharmacy, Daimler Chrysler, Express Employment Professionals, Federal Reserve Bank of Chicago, 5th 3rd Bank, Folgers Coffee, General Motors, Hewlett Packard, Ideas of America, Mc Donald's, Moorings Park, Ohio Housing Association, Onyx Benefits Group, Paranet Group, Pekin Insurance, Radio Shack, Raymond James, Re Max, RMA Land Construction, Securities and Licensing Association, Smuckers, State Farm Insurance, Sun Life Financial, Taco Bell and Verizon Wireless.

EDUCATION:

Ann Arbor Public Schools, Chicago Public Schools, Consortium of Mid-Michigan Instructional Teams (C.O.M.M.I.T.), Connections Conference, Covert Public Schools, Detroit Public Schools, Eastern Michigan University, Flint Public Schools, Lawrence P. Doss Scholarship Foundation, Illinois Connections Conference, Illinois State University, Kellogg Community College, Michigan Institute for Educational Management, Michigan State University, National Association of Black Educators, National School Board Association, Prime Time Palm Beach County After School Symposium, Penn State University, Saginaw Public Schools, Saginaw Valley State, Southern Seven Health Department, Stanislaus County Office of Education, Texas Southern University, Wayne County Community

College, Wayne County Neighbor Legal Services, Wayne State University, Wisconsin Student Achievement Network, Wyoming Public School District, University of Detroit, University of Michigan Meeting Planners, University of Phoenix, University of Wisconsin Madison

GOVERNMENT:

Cap Lake County Child Care Community Services, Career Works, Inc, Community Action Partnership of Lake County, Detroit Water and Sewage, Facilities Operators Directors Conference, FBI, Illinois Department on Aging, Illinois State Advisory Council on Education, Macomb County Department of Human Services, Michigan Department of Community Health, Michigan Office of Recipient Rights, Michigan School Business Officials, Michigan Society of Governmental Meeting Planners, North Carolina Work Force Development, Omaha Public Power District, OSHA (Michigan), Pontiac Public Library, Society of Government Meeting Planners-Michigan SGMP, Starfish Family Services, Veterans Administration, Virginia Association of Housing Community, United States Department of Insurance, Securities and Banking.

We understand that you're conducting a lecture series around the book can you explain?

Yes, it's something that I'm really excited to offer this year! The lecture series allows us to travel the country and share our message live with hundreds of thousands of people that would not ordinarily have the opportunity. We have partnered with hundreds of libraries, school districts, universities, community colleges and non profits to make it possible. More details are available at **www.jonathanedison.com**

SHARE **SURVIVAL MODE**

Who else do you know that is in Survival Mode? Make a list of co-workers, friends and family members that need to be inspired, motivated and reassured. Once you complete your list- Email, call and/or text them the title "Survival Mode" and encourage them to order a copy today!

1. _____

2. _____

3. _____

4. _____

5. _____

6. _____

7. _____

8. _____

9. _____

10. _____

11. _____

12. _____

13. _____

14. _____

15. _____

Do you want to
BOOK JONATHAN NOW,
or invite him to your Book Club?

Visit **www.jonathaedison.com** or scan the QR Code below.

If someone wanted to book you to speak, set up a book signing or invite you to host a lecture series how would they get in touch with you?

That's an easy one:
They can simply call our office at **1-972-755-4231** or visit us on the web **www.jonathanedison.com** and fill out the
BOOK JONATHAN FORM

JONATHAN EDISON